COGAT®
GRADE 3 & GRADE 4

2 Practice Tests
Level 9 and 10

Savant Test Prep™

www.SavantPrep.com

Please leave a review for this book!

Thank you for purchasing this resource.

Please take a moment to leave a
review on the website where you purchased this.

TABLE OF CONTENTS

INTRODUCTION

COGAT® GENERAL INFORMATION

- COGAT® stands for Cognitive Abilities Test®.
- The test measures students' reasoning skills and problem-solving skills.
- It provides educators with an overall assessment of students' academic strengths and weaknesses.
- The COGAT® is commonly used as a screener for gifted and talented programs.
    - Gifted and Talented (G&T) selection sometimes requires a teacher recommendation as well.
- The test is usually administered in a group setting.
- A teacher (or other school associate) administers the test, reading the directions.
- Please check with your school/testing site regarding its testing procedures, as these may differ.

COGAT® LEVEL 9 AND LEVEL 10 FORMAT

- Students in third grade take the COGAT® Level 9. Students in fourth grade take the COGAT® Level 10.
- The test for third grade has 170 questions. The test for fourth grade has 176 questions.
- The test is divided into 3 main parts, each called a "Battery." Each Battery has three question types. See the chart below.

VERBAL BATTERY	NON-VERBAL BATTERY	QUANTITATIVE BATTERY
Verbal Analogies: 22 Questions*	Figure Analogies: 20 Questions*	Number Puzzles: 16 Questions
Verbal Classification: 20 Questions	Figure Classification: 20 Questions*	Number Series: 18 Questions
Sentence Completion: 20 Questions	Paper Folding: 16 Questions	Number Analogies: 18 Questions

*The fourth grade test has an additional two questions for Verbal Analogies, Figure Analogies, and Figure Classification.

- Often, schools administer one Battery per day, allowing approximately 45 minutes per Battery.
- Students have around 15 minutes to complete each question type (for example, students would have around 15 minutes to complete Verbal Analogies).
- See the following pages for examples and explanations of each question type.

COGAT® SCORING

- Students receive points for correct answers. Points are not deducted for incorrect answers. (Therefore, students should at least guess versus leaving a question blank.)
- In general, schools have a "cut-off" COGAT® score, which they consider together with additional criteria, for gifted & talented acceptance. This varies by school.
- This score is usually at least 98%. (However, some schools accept scores of 95% or even 85%.)
- A score of 98% means that your child scored as well as, or better than, 98% of those in his/her testing group.
- COGAT® scores are available for the entire test and can be broken down by Battery.
- Depending on the school/program, such a "cut-off" score may only be required on one or two of the Batteries (and not on the test overall).
- It is essential to check with your school/program for their acceptance procedures.
- The COGAT® Practice Tests in this book can not yield these percentiles because they have not been given to a large enough group of students to produce an accurate comparison/calculation.

HOW TO USE THIS BOOK

1. Go over the Question Examples together with your child. These begin on the next page.

2. Do Practice Test 1 (Workbook Format).
   - Do these questions with your child, especially if this is your child's first exposure to COGAT®-prep questions. These questions have a "workbook format," meaning they are meant to be done together.
   - Do not assign a time limit.
   - Talk about what the question is asking your child to do.
   - Questions progress in difficulty. (The first few questions are quite simple.)
   - Go over the answers using the Answer Key.
   - For questions missed, go over the answers again, discussing what makes the correct answer better than the other choices.

3. Do Practice Test 2.
   - If your child progressed easily through Practice Test 1, see how well they can do without your help.
   - If your child needed assistance with much of Practice Test 1, then continue to assist your child with Practice Test 2.
   - If you wish to assign a time limit, assign around 15 minutes per question type.
   - Go over the answers using the Answer Key.
   - For questions missed, go over the answers again, discussing what makes the correct answer better than the other choices.

4. Need more practice?

   - **Get 300+ new questions per book.**

   - **Check out Savant Test Prep™ books on Amazon®.**

TEST-TAKING TIPS

- Ensure your child listens carefully to the directions, especially in the Sentence Completion section.
- Make sure (s)he does not rush through questions. (There is no prize for finishing first!) Tell your child to look carefully at the question. Then, tell your child to look at each answer choice before marking his/her answer.
  - If you notice your child continuing to rush through the questions, tell him/her to point to each part of the question. Then, point to each answer choice.
- If (s)he does not know the answer, then use the process of elimination. Cross out any answer choices which are clearly incorrect, then choose from those remaining.
- This tip/suggestion is entirely at your discretion. You may wish to offer some sort of special motivation to encourage your child to do his/her best. An extra incentive of, for example, an art set, a building block set, or a special outing can go a long way in motivating young learners!
- The night before testing, make sure your child has enough sleep, without any interruptions. (Think about the difference in **your** brain function with a good night's sleep vs. without. The same goes for your child's.)
- The morning before the test, ensure your child eats a healthy breakfast with protein and complex carbs. Do not let them eat sugar, chocolate, etc.
- If you can choose the time your child will take the test (for example, if (s)he will take the test individually, instead of at school with a group), opt for a morning testing session, when your child will be most alert.

QUESTION EXAMPLES

- Here is an overview of the COGAT® question types.
- This section has <u>simple</u> examples, to introduce your child to test concepts.
    - Do these examples together with your child.
- Below the questions are explanations for parents.

1. VERBAL ANALOGIES (VERBAL BATTERY)

• **Directions:** Here are two sets of words. Look at the first set of words. Try to see how they belong together. Then, look at the next set of words. The question mark shows where the answer is missing. Can you see which answer choice would make the second set of words go together in the same way that the first set of words goes together?

scales → fish : feathers → ?   A. pen   B. shark   C. beak   D. bird   E. fly

• **Explanation:** Figure out how the first set is related and belongs together. Then, (s)he must figure out which answer choice would go with the first word of the second set so that the second set would have the same analogous relationship as the first set. (The small arrows demonstrate that the words go together.)

• **Strategy 1:** Define a "rule" to describe how the first set belongs together. Then, take this "rule" and use it with the second set. Look at the answer choices, and figure out which answer would make the second set follow your "rule."

In this question, we have "scales" and "fish." Scales are part of a fish. Also, more specifically, scales cover a fish. A rule would be, "the first thing covers the second thing." In the second set, we have "feathers." Let's try the answer choices with our rule. A pen, shark, beak, or fly is not correct. "Bird" is correct because feathers cover a bird.

• **Strategy 2:** Come up with a sentence to describe how the first set belongs together. Then, use this sentence with the second word. Look at the answer choices, and figure out which answer would make the sentence work with this second set. With both strategies, if more than one answer choice works, then you need a more specific rule/sentence.

• Make sure your child does not choose an answer simply because it *has to do with* the previous words or reminds them of previous words. In the above example, "beak" *has to do with* "feathers." "Shark" may *remind* them of the second word in the first set, "fish." These types of words are sometimes included in the answer choices, and students who do not look carefully at the question may choose them by mistake.

• The examples on the next page outline some of the logic used in analogy questions.

• **Directions:** The first set of words goes together in some way. In the second set of words, one word is missing. Which answer choice would make the second set of words go together in the same way that the first set goes together? (Note: the answer and logic are below the question.)

Question	Answer Choices			
1. Spider -is to- Web as Bird -is to- ? *Answer - Nest (Animal: Animal's Home)*	Flower	Bench	Nest	Bird
2. Acorns -are to- Squirrel as Seeds -are to- ? *Answer - Bird (Animal: Animal's Food)*	Grass	Bird	Fish	Snake
3. Calf -is to- Cow as Cub -is to- ? *Answer - Tiger (Animal Baby: Animal Adult)*	Tiger	Horse	Goose	Bull
4. Small -is to- Little as Afraid -is to- ? *Answer - Scared (Synonyms)*	Dark	Tired	Haunted	Scared
5. Happy -is to- Sad as Wet -is to- ? *Answer - Dry (Opposites)*	Damp	Clean	Water	Dry
6. Tiger -is to- Cheetah as Butterfly -is to- ? *Answer - Moth (Similar: Similar (Flying Insects))*	Bird	Bat	Moth	Jaguar
7. Flower -is to- Bouquet as Kernel -is to- ? *Answer - Corn Cob (Part: Whole)*	Snack	Plant	Corn Cob	Crop
8. Ship -is to- Port as Car -is to- ? *Answer - Garage (Object: Location)*	Truck	Garage	Marina	Wheel
9. Pencil -is to- Paper as Paint -is to- ? *Answer - Wall (Object: Object Used With)*	Wall	Color	Red	Light
10. Lumber -is to- Fence as Paper -is to- ? *Answer - Book (Object: Product That Object Is Put Together To Make)*	Log	Branch	Tree	Book
11. Cheese -is to- Refrigerator as Ice -is to- ? *Answer - Freezer (Object: Item Used to Store/Hold Object)*	Snow	Toaster	Freezer	Cube
12. Box -is to- Cube as Globe -is to- ? *Answer - Sphere (Object: Similar Shape)*	Prism	Sphere	Oval	Pentagon
13. Straw -is to- Juice as Spoon -is to- ? *Answer - Cereal (Utensil: Object Utensil Is Used With)*	Cereal	Salad	Steak	Sandwich
14. Egg -is to- Chicken as Milk -is to- ? *Answer - Cow (Food/Drink: Source of Food/Drink)*	Chick	Cheese	Rooster	Cow
15. Ambulance -is to- Paramedic as Tractor -is to- ? *Answer - Farmer (Object/Vehicle: User)*	Doctor	Teacher	Scientist	Farmer
16. Large -is to- Enormous as Good -is to- ? *Answer - Super (Adjective: Higher Degree of Adjective)*	Bad	So-so	Happy	Super
17. Rose -is to- Flower as Ant -is to- ? *Answer - Insect (Specific Type: Group)*	Insect	Spider	Anthill	Beetle

2. VERBAL CLASSIFICATION (VERBAL BATTERY)

• **Directions:** The three words in the top row are alike in some way. Look at the bottom row. There are five words. Which word in the bottom row goes best with the three words in the top row?

red   green   blue

A. paint	B. color	C. white	D. rainbow	E. shade

• **Explanation:** Together with your child, try to figure out a "rule" describing how the top words are alike and belong together. Then, apply the "rule" to each answer choice to determine which one follows it. If your child finds that more than one choice follows the rule, then a more specific rule is needed.

• **Using the above question as an example, say to your child:** In the top row, we have "red," "green," and "blue." What do these have in common? Each of these are colors. This is how they are alike. Which answer choice follows this rule of "colors?" The only answer choice that does is "white."

• Make sure your child does not choose a word simply because the choice *has to do with* the top three. For example, the other choices, especially Choice B ("color") have to do with the top three. However, "white" is the only choice that actually follows the rule.

Here is another example to demonstrate the importance of "rules" that are *specific*.

Atlantic   Indian   Arctic

A. American	B. Caribbean Sea	C. East Coast	D. Pacific	E. ocean

In this example, the correct rule is "oceans of the world." (The world's oceans are the: Atlantic, Pacific, Arctic, Indian, and Southern.)

However, a test-taker may at first come up with the rule "large body of water." If this happens, (s)he would have more than one answer choice that could be correct (Caribbean Sea or Pacific).

In this case, a more specific rule is needed. Here, (s)he should read the top three words again. In doing so, (s)he may realize that the top three words are large bodies of water that are *also* oceans.

A more specific rule would be "ocean" or "oceans of the world." Therefore, the correct answer would be Choice D, "Pacific."

• **Directions:** The first 3 words go together in some way. Let's figure out how the words go together. Next, is a group of 4 words. Let's figure out which one from this group goes best with the words in the first group.

(Parent note: the answer and logic are below the question.)

Question				Answer Choices			
1. Cave	Hive	Web		Spider	Nest	Vet	Bat

Answer - Nest (Animal Homes)

2. Butterfly	Ant	Bee		Worm	Horse	Bird	Dragonfly

Answer - Dragonfly (Animal Types (Insects))

3. Forest	Jungle	Desert		Tree	Valley	Rainforest	City

Answer - Rainforest (Habitats)

4. Lemon	Grape	Apple		Strawberry	Farm	Sweet	Lettuce

Answer - Strawberry (Kinds of Food (Fruit))

5. Scientist	Nurse	Detective		Superhero	Teenager	Pilot	Fairy

Answer - Pilot (Jobs)

6. Sock	Skate	Boot		Slipper	Cap	Mitten	Toe

Answer - Slipper (Objects Worn On Feet)

7. Hot Air Balloon	Jet	Helicopter		Ship	Airport	Bird	Airplane

Answer - Airplane (Vehicles for Air Travel)

8. Ruler	Measuring Tape	Scale		Thermometer	TV	Pen	Number

Answer - Thermometer (Object Use (Used to Measure))

9. Pillow	Blanket	Mattress		Towel	Chair	Sheet	Table

Answer - Sheet (Object Location (Found on Beds))

10. Fire	Sun	Stove		Cookie	Toaster	Beach	Camp

Answer - Toaster (Object Characteristics (Provide Heat))

11. Planet	Ball	Globe		Country	Goal	Bubble	Racetrack

Answer - Bubble (Object Shape (Spherical))

3. SENTENCE COMPLETION (VERBAL BATTERY)

• **Directions:** First, read the sentence. There is a missing word. Which answer choice goes best in the sentence? (Read the sentences and choices to your child. They may read along silently.)

As the water slowly evaporated, the bird bath became _____.

A. wet   B. empty   C. full   D. damp   E. clean

• **Explanation** Here, your child must use the information in the question and make inferences (i.e., make a best guess based on the information) and choose the *best* answer choice to fill in the blank.

• Note that Sentence Completion questions do not solely test vocabulary, but reasoning skills as well.

• Make sure your child pays close attention to every word in the sentence and to every answer choice. Have him/her re-read the complete sentence with the answer choice to ensure their choice makes the *most* sense compared to the other choices (the answer is B).

•Tell him/her to pay special attention to "negative" words like "not" or "no." Also, (s)he should watch out for words like "though," "although," "even though," which would show contrasting ideas.

4. FIGURE ANALOGIES (NON-VERBAL BATTERY)

• **Directions:** The pictures in the top boxes go together in some way. Look at the bottom boxes. One box is empty. Look at the row of pictures next to the boxes. These are the answer choices. Which one of these choices goes with the picture in the bottom box like the pictures in the top box go together?

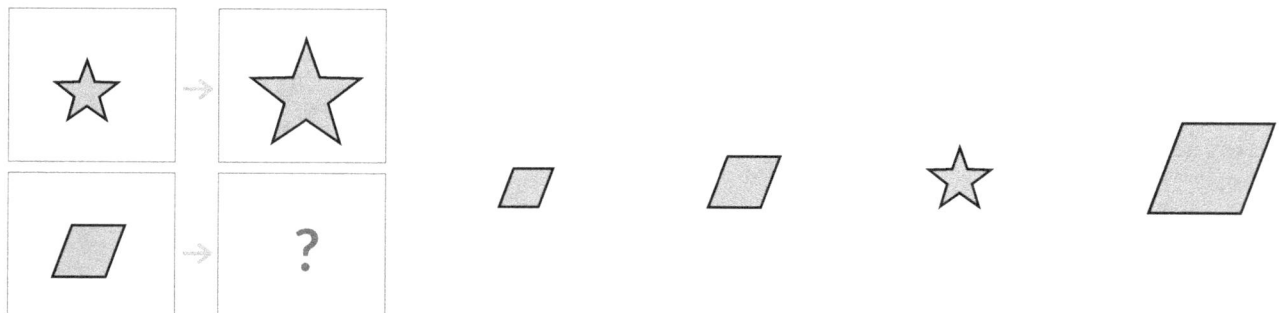

• **Explanation:** In the directions, the word "picture" means a "figure" consisting of one or more shapes/lines/etc. As with Verbal Analogies, try to define a "rule" to describe how the top set belongs together.

With Figure Analogies, however, make your "rule" describe a "change" that occurs from the top left box to the top right box. Next, take this "rule" describing the change, and apply it to the bottom picture.

Then, look at the answer choices to determine which one would make the bottom set also follow your "rule."

• In the top left box, we see 1 star. In the top right box, we also see a star, but it has gotten bigger. Let's come up with a rule to describe how the picture has changed from left to right. From left to right, the shape gets bigger. On the bottom is a parallelogram. Let's look at the answer choices and see if any fit our rule. The first choice does not - the shape is smaller. The second choice does not - the shape is the same size. The third choice does not - it is a different shape. The last choice does - it is the same shape as the bottom box, but it is bigger.

• Basic questions, like the example, have one "change."
• More advanced questions, like #10-12 below, have two changes (or changes that are not as obvious).

Directions for the below images.
• See if your child can figure out how the first picture "changes" to the second picture below.
• The questions' "change" (the logic) is at the bottom of the page.

1.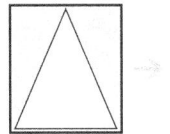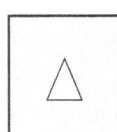

2.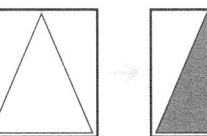

3.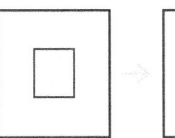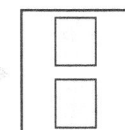

4.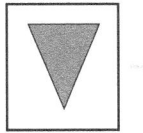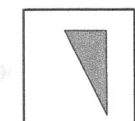

5.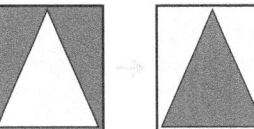

6.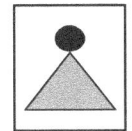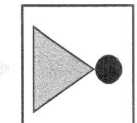

7.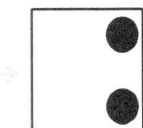

8.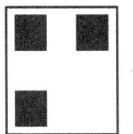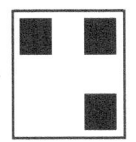

9.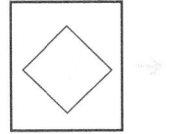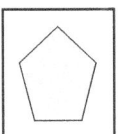

10.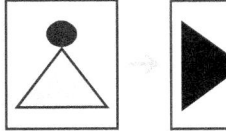

11.

12.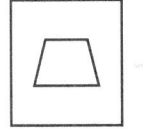

1. Size (gets smaller)
2. Color (white to dark gray)
3. Quantity (plus 1)
4. Whole to Half
5. Color Reversal
6. Rotation (clockwise, 90°)

7. Rotation (clockwise, 90°)
8. Rotation -or- Mirror Image/"Flip"
9. Number of Shape Sides (shape with +1 side)
10. Two Changes: Rotation (clockwise, 90°) and Color Reversal
11. Two Changes: Shape Position and Size
12. Two Changes: Shape Size and Color

11

5. FIGURE CLASSIFICATION (NON-VERBAL BATTERY)

• **Directions:** The top row shows three pictures that are alike in some way. Look at the bottom row. There are four pictures. Which picture in the bottom row goes best with the pictures in the top row?

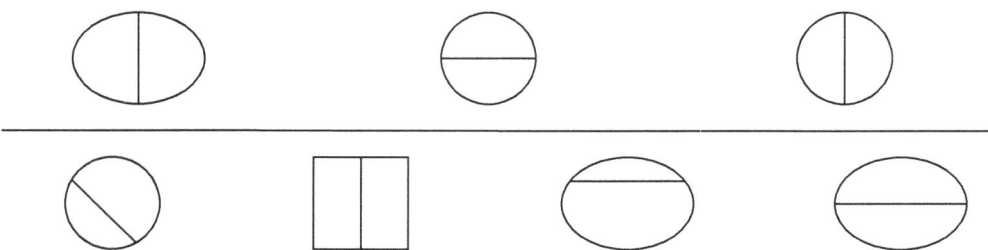

• **Explanation:** Together with your child, try to figure out a "rule" describing how the top pictures are alike and belong together. Then, apply the "rule" to each answer choice to determine which one follows it. If your child finds that more than one choice follows the rule, then a more specific rule is needed.

• Here we see 1 oval divided in half, 1 circle divided in half, and 1 circle divided in half. What is a rule that describes how they are alike? They are all round and divided in half. In the bottom row, which choice follows this rule? Choice 1 and 3 are round and divided, but not divided in half. Choice 2 is divided in half, but it is not round. Choice 4 is round and divided in half.

• The following examples include basic logic used in Figure Classification questions, with answers at the end.

• **Directions:** The top row shows three pictures that are alike in some way. Look at the bottom row. There are four pictures. Which picture in the bottom row goes best with the pictures in the top row?

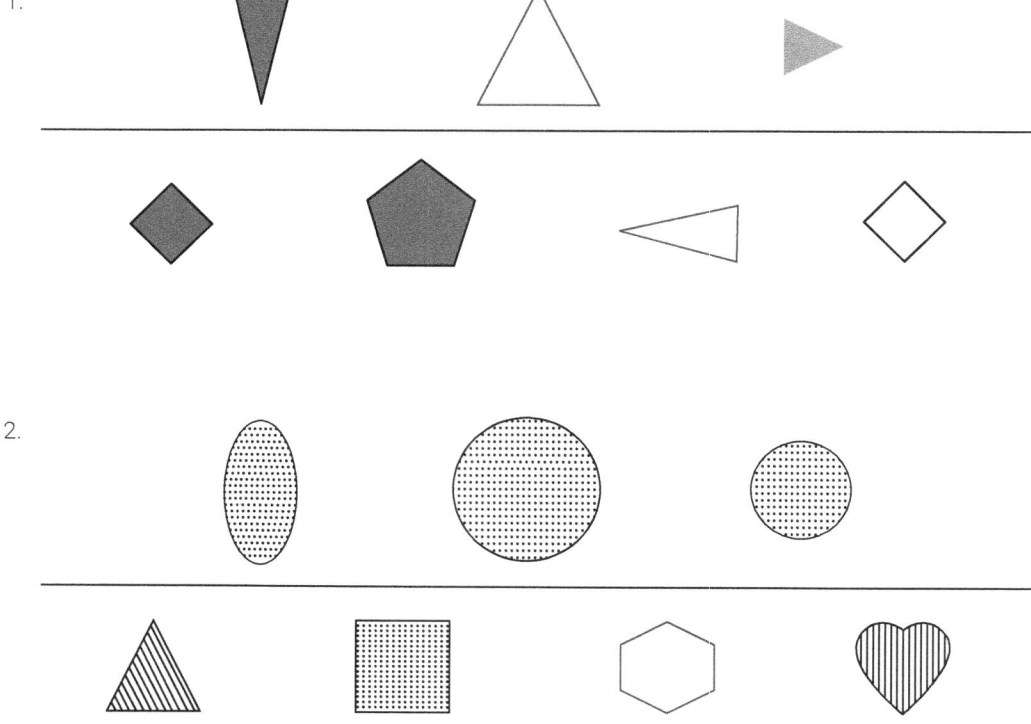

• **Note:** These are <u>more challenging</u>. If your child needs help, ask them the question next to the number.

3. Which way is it pointing?

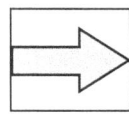  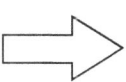

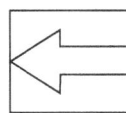 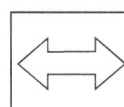 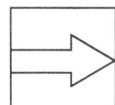 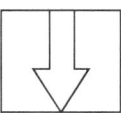

4. What is the design inside?

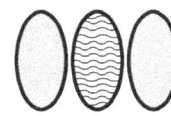  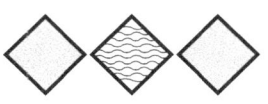

 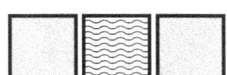 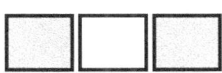 

5. How much is black? How much is white?

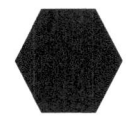   

6. How many sides?

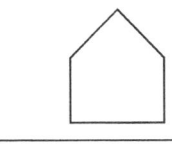 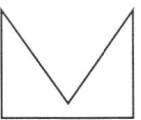 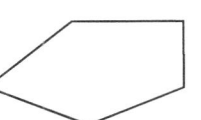

   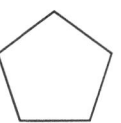

1- Choice 3: triangles   2- Choice 2: filled with dots   3- Choice 3: arrows point right
4- Choice 2: the designs are gray, wavy lines, gray   5- Choice 2: half is white, half is black
6- Choice 4: the shapes have 5 sides

7. How many shapes of each kind are together next to each other?

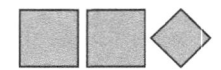 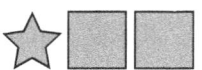 

8. What kind of small shapes are there?

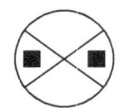  

9. What kinds of shape are gray or white? How many?

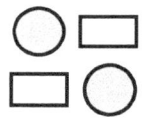 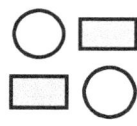 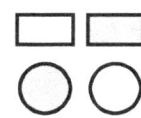 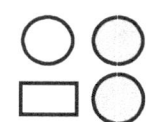

10. How many shapes are in each group?

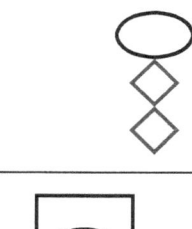  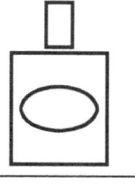

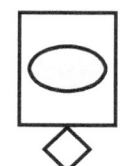  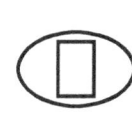 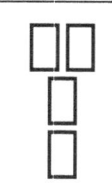

7-Choice 3: there are 2 identical shapes next to a shape that's a different kind of shape
8-Choice 4: the 2 small black shapes are the same
9-Choice 3: the 2 gray shapes are 1 rectangle and 1 circle   10-Choice 1: there are 3 shapes in the group

14

6. PAPER FOLDING (NON-VERBAL BATTERY)

• **Directions:** The top row of pictures shows a sheet of paper. The paper was folded, then something was cut out. Which picture in the bottom row shows how the paper would look after it's unfolded?

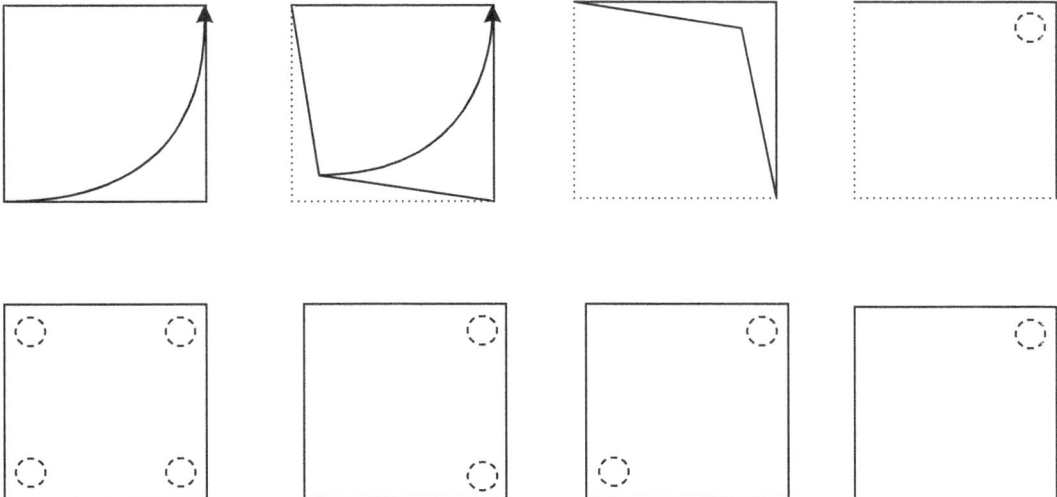

• **Explanation:** The first choice has too many holes. In the second choice, the holes are not in the correct position. The third choice has the correct number of holes and in the correct position. The last choice only shows the hole on top.

• **Tip:** If Paper Folding is challenging for your child, demonstrate using real paper and scissors. (It is common for kids to initially struggle with Paper Folding. It is not an activity most children have much experience with.)

• Show your child the following examples. Demonstrate using real paper, if needed.

Paper Folding Steps   Result

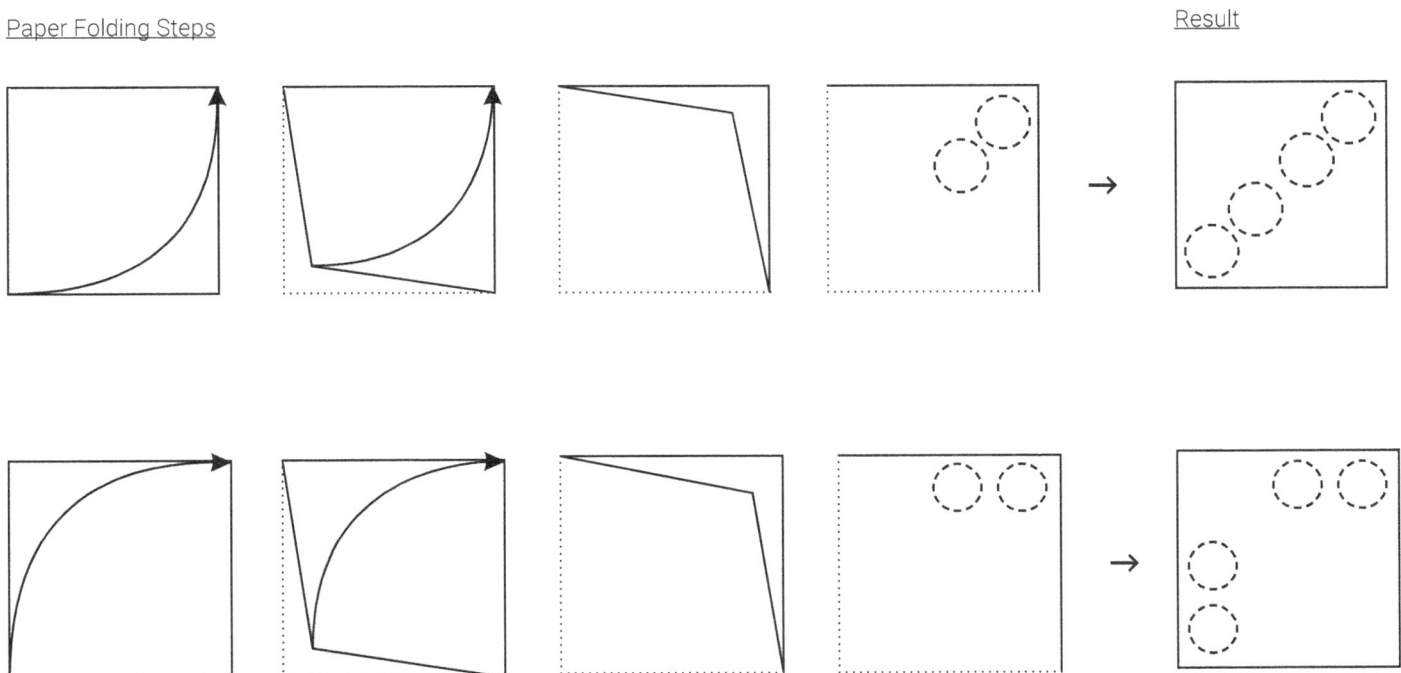

(In the question at the top of the page, the third choice is correct.)

In the example below, point out to your child that when the paper is unfolded the triangles point toward each other.

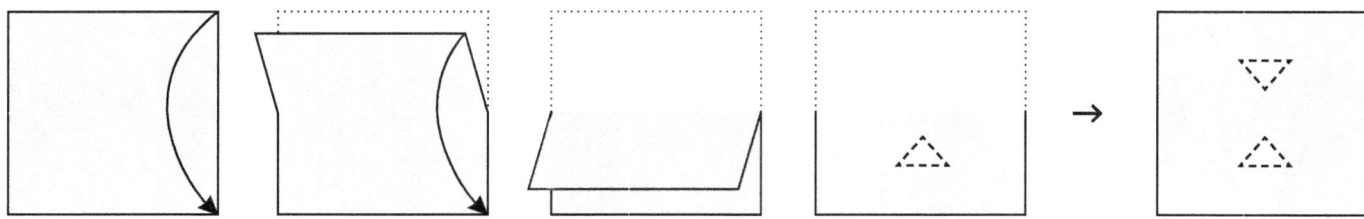

In the example below, point out to your child that the shape is cut into the fold line.

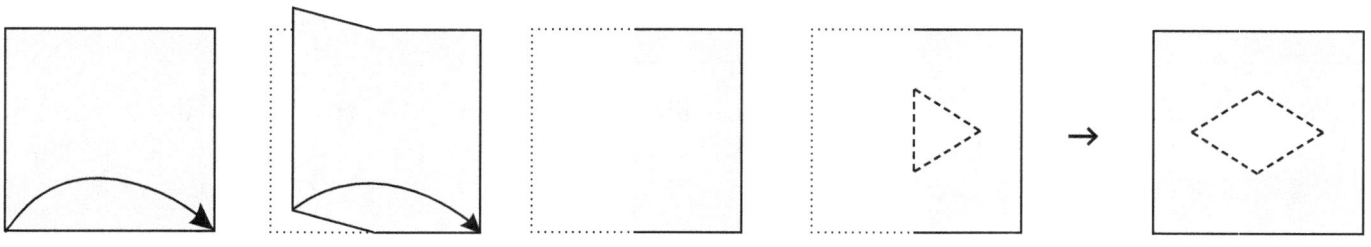

In the examples below, point out to your child how the paper is folded, and then folded again.

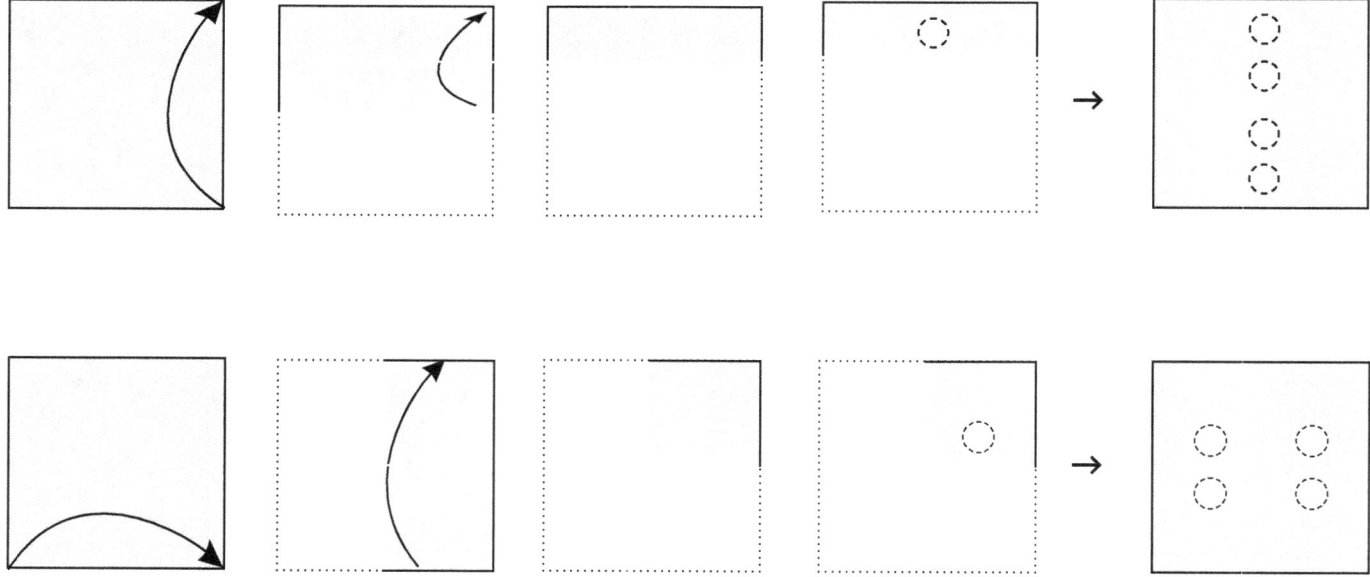

7. NUMBER PUZZLES (QUANTITATIVE BATTERY)

• **Directions:** What goes in place of the question mark so that both sides of the equal sign are the same?

• **Explanation:** These questions have two formats. The first example is a standard math problem. In the second example, your child needs to replace the black shape with the given number. Should your child have problems figuring out the answer of either format, (s)he can simply test each answer choice until they find the correct answer. The answer to #1 is E. The answer to #2 is D.

1. $19 = ? + 5$ A. 5   B. 24   C. 20   D. 4   E. 14

2. $? = \blacklozenge - 8$ A. 0   B. 1   C. 2   D. 3   E. 4

    $\blacklozenge = 11$

8A. NUMBER SERIES (QUANTITATIVE BATTERY), TEXT FORMAT

• **Directions:** The top row of numbers have made a pattern. Which answer choice would complete the pattern?

• **Number Format Explanation:** To help your child see the pattern, ask them to write the difference between each number and the next. Here, the difference between 6 and 9 is 3. The difference between 9 and 12 is 3. The difference between 12 and 15 is 3, and so on. In less challenging questions, this "difference" will be the same for each set of numbers. If the pattern is "add 3," then the answer is 21, because 18 +3 = 21.

6   9   12   15   18   ?

A. 21   B. 3   C. 22   D. 24   E. 30

In more challenging questions, this pattern is not consistent with each set of numbers. See below:

| 30 | 29 | 27 | 24 | 20 | 15 | ? | Pattern: -1, -2, -3, -4, etc.; Answer: 9 |

| 7 | 2 | 1 | 7 | 2 | 1 | ? | Pattern: 7 - 2 - 1; Answer: 7 |

| 3 | 4 | 6 | 7 | 9 | 10 | ? | Pattern: +1, +2, +1, +2, etc; Answer: 12 |

| 5 | 0 | 6 | 0 | 7 | 0 | ? | Pattern: every other number +1; every other number = 0; Answer: 8 |

8B. NUMBER SERIES (QUANTITATIVE BATTERY), ABACUS FORMAT

• **Directions:** Which rod should go in the place of the missing rod to finish the pattern?

• **Explanation for #1:** Before the missing rod, the other rods have made a pattern that we need to figure out. Then, we will complete the pattern with the correct answer choice. From left to right, we see that the pattern is: 1 - 2 - 1 - 2 - 1. After 1, comes 2. This means that the missing rod needs 2 beads.

• Make sure your child accurately counts the number of beads. In the examples below, there are numbers under the rods indicating the number of beads. The practice test questions do not have these numbers.

• After you do #1, go over questions #2 - #7 together. The pattern and the answer are already given.

1.

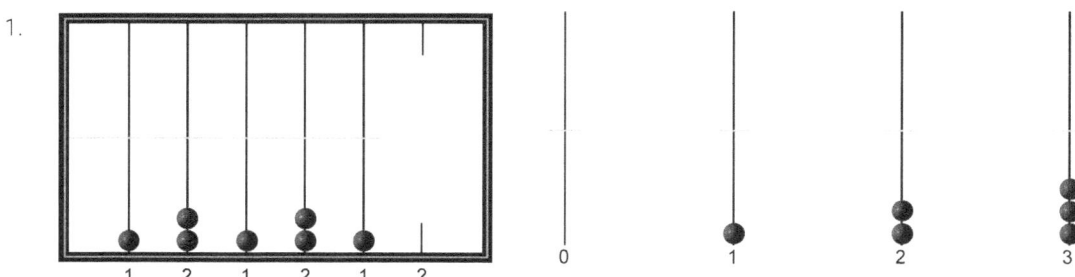

Pattern: the number of beads decreases by 1. The answer is 1.

2.

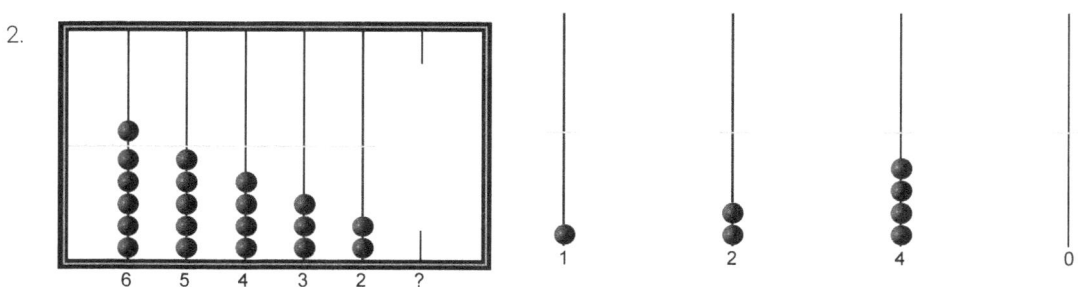

Pattern: every other rod increases by 1. And, the alternate rods equal 0. The answer is 0.

3.

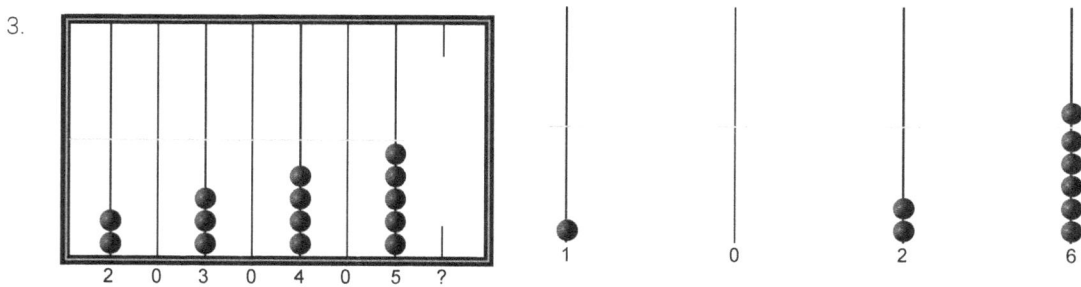

Pattern: the rods repeat 7 - 5 - 3. The answer is 7.

4.

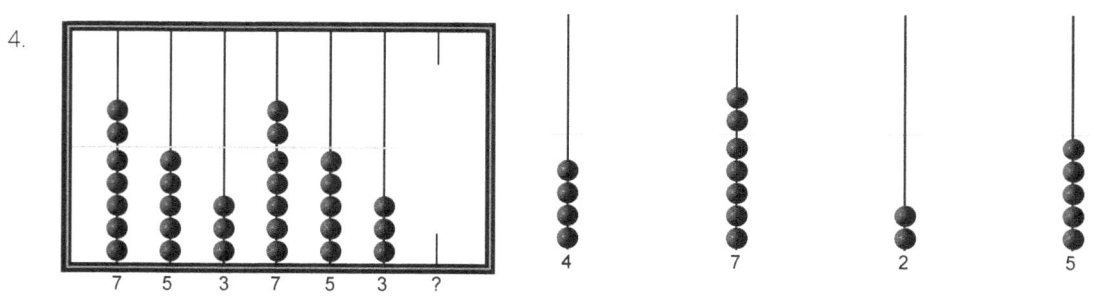

Every other rod increases by one (1 - 2 - 3 - 4). Then, every other rod (the alternate rods), increases by one (4 - 5 - 6 - 7). With the alternating rods increasing 1, 2, 3, 4, this means that the next rod will be 5.

5.

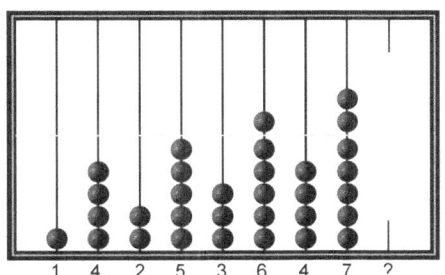

Every other rod decreases by one (5 - 4 - 3). Then, every other rod (the alternate rods), increases by one (1 - 2 - 3). With the alternating rods decreasing 5, 4, 3, this means that the next rod will be 2.

6.

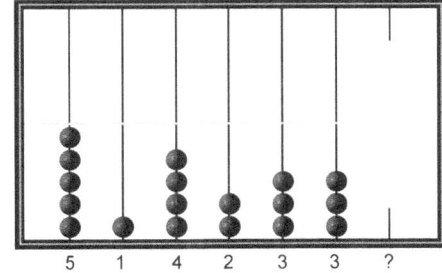

Pattern: the rods decrease with the pattern 6 - 4 - 2 - 0, then increase with the reverse pattern 2 - 4 - 6.

7.

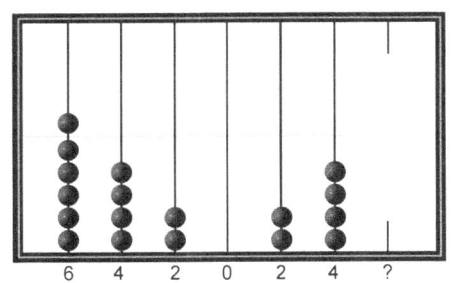

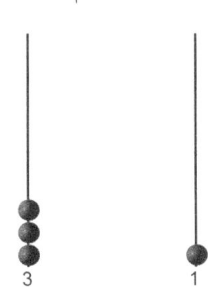

9A. NUMBER ANALOGIES (QUANTITATIVE BATTERY), FORMAT 1

• **Directions:** Look at the first two sets of numbers. Come up with a rule that both of these sets follow. Use this rule to figure out which answer choice goes in place of the question mark in the last set of numbers.

• **Explanation:** Have your child figure out a rule that explains how the first number "changes" into the second number. It could use addition, subtraction, multiplication, or division. Have him/her write the rule by *each* pair. (S)he must make sure this rule works with *both* pairs. The rule for the first question is "+4," so 33 is the answer.

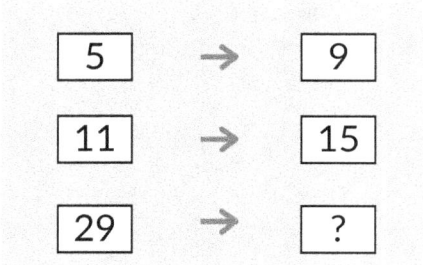

A. 25   B. 33   C. 4   D. 24   E. 32

9B. NUMBER ANALOGIES (QUANTITATIVE BATTERY), FORMAT 2

• **Directions:** Look at the first two sets of numbers. Come up with a rule that both of these sets follow. Use this rule to figure out which answer choice goes in place of the question mark in the last set of numbers.

• **Explanation:** In the first set, it may appear that the rule is "add 4," because 2 + 4 = 6. However, looking at the second set, you see that this rule does not work. Let's go back to first set. How else can you go from 2 to 6? You can multiply: 2 x 3 = 6. Let's try the rule "multiply by 3." Apply this rule to the second set: 4 x 3 = 12. The rule "multiply by 3" works in both sets. In the third set, 10 x 3 = 30 (choice D).

[2 → 6]   [4 → 12]   [10 → ?]   A. 6   B. 3   C. 13   D. 30   E. 7

Read this before you start.

Watch out!

This book is filled with tricky questions. Can you answer them?

Of course you can!

Pay close attention to each question and try your best.

We'll be here to help you along the way!

COGAT® PRACTICE TEST 1
(WORKBOOK FORMAT)

VERBAL ANALOGIES

What's missing?

Sara

Directions (Read these aloud to your child. Your child may read along silently): The first set of words goes together in some way. In the second set of words, one word is missing. You must figure out which answer choice would go in place of the question mark so that the second set of words goes together in the same way that the first set of words goes together.

Explanation (for parents): A more detailed explanation and another example question is on p.6. If you have not already, look over p.6. Following is an excerpt. Your child must figure out how the first set of words is related and belongs together. Then, (s)he must figure out which answer choice would replace the question mark so that the second set would have the same relationship as the first set.

Example (read this to child): "Eye" and "see." These are the words in the first set. (Together, try to come up with a "rule" or a sentence describing how they are alike and go together.) You use your eye to see. A person uses the first word to do the second word. Let's look at the next set. The first word is "ear." Next, let's carefully look at each answer choice. Remembering our rule or our sentence, which choice goes best with "ear?" What do you use your ear to do? "Hear." A person uses their ear to hear (choice D).

1   **eye → see : ear → ?**

   A earring   B head   C smell   D hear   E headphones

2   **tiger → mammal : ostrich → ?**

   A bird   B eagle   C lion   D feather   E animal

3 disk → circle : dice → ?

  ^{A} game ^{B} cube ^{C} dot ^{D} roll ^{E} pair

4 corn → stalk : grapes → ?

  ^{A} bunch ^{B} juice ^{C} vine ^{D} seed ^{E} root

5 distance → meter : weight → ?

  ^{A} scale ^{B} heavy ^{C} number ^{D} height ^{E} gram

6 carpenter → wood : gardener → ?

  ^{A} rake ^{B} plants ^{C} shovel ^{D} green ^{E} path

7 skin → human : bark → ?

  ^{A} leaf ^{B} tree ^{C} sap ^{D} dog ^{E} forest

8   Africa → Nile : South America → ?

      (A) Andes   (B) Amazon   (C) river   (D) Brazil   (E) Pacific

9   building → basement : volcano → ?

      (A) crater   (B) eruption   (C) lava   (D) ash   (E) smoke

10   sparrow → eagle : salmon → ?

      (A) shrimp   (B) squid   (C) frog   (D) shark   (E) octopus

11   victory → defeat : truth → ?

      (A) believe   (B) honest   (C) lie   (D) speech   (E) explain

12   carrot → broccoli : peach → ?

      (A) tree   (B) fruit   (C) pie   (D) apple   (E) yellow

13   **snake → reptile : toad → ?**

     A amphibian   B mammal   C fish   D insect   E frog

14   **biplane → jet : canoe → ?**

     A cruise ship   B spaceship   C paddle   D raft   E river

15   **saw → tree : knife → ?**

     A chair   B oak   C bread   D pine   E ax

16   **cotton → shirt : rubber → ?**

     A tire   B glue   C plastic   D chair   E pants

17   **single → one : quadruple → ?**

     A three   B five   C quarter   D four   E quadrant

18   house   → attic : mountain → ?

    Ⓐ base   Ⓑ summit   Ⓒ trail   Ⓓ valley   Ⓔ range

19   identical   → opposite : frigid → ?

    Ⓐ chilly   Ⓑ refrigerator   Ⓒ oven   Ⓓ tropical   Ⓔ mild

20   novel   → author : sculpture → ?

    Ⓐ model   Ⓑ statue   Ⓒ painter   Ⓓ museum   Ⓔ sculptor

Good job!
Let's do some more!

Caleb

VERBAL CLASSIFICATION

Which one goes best?

Kai

Directions (Read these aloud to your child. Your child may read along silently): The top row has three words that are alike in some way. In the bottom row are five words. Which word in the bottom row goes best with the words in the top row?

Explanation (for parents): A more detailed explanation and another Verbal Classification example question is on p.8. If you have not already, look over p.8. Following is an excerpt. Together with your child, try to figure out a "rule" describing how the top words are alike and belong together. Then, apply the "rule" to each answer choice to determine which one follows it. If your child finds that more than one choice follows the rule, then a more specific rule is needed.

Example: In the top row are the words "robin," "sparrow," and "falcon." Let's come up with a "rule" to describe how these are each alike or how they belong together. These are all types of birds. Now, let's look carefully at each answer choice and remember our rule of "birds." "Hawk" follows our rule because it is a type of bird. (Note that if you had a rule of "things that fly," it would not be specific enough. A bat, butterfly, and hawk all fly. So, you would need a rule that is more specific.) The correct answer is choice C.

1   **robin   sparrow   falcon**

   A bat   B butterfly   C hawk   D kangaroo   E beaver

2   **violin   cello   harp**

   A horn   B instrument   C trumpet   D drums   E guitar

3   **essay**   **article**   **report**

Ⓐ fiction   Ⓑ library   Ⓒ fairy tale   Ⓓ biography   Ⓔ fantasy

4   **frying**   **baking**   **grilling**

Ⓐ chopping   Ⓑ mixing   Ⓒ washing   Ⓓ eating   Ⓔ boiling

5   **notebook**   **easel**   **paper**

Ⓐ chair   Ⓑ chalkboard   Ⓒ marker   Ⓓ eraser   Ⓔ pencil

6   **t-shirt**   **shorts**   **flip-flops**

Ⓐ tank top   Ⓑ scarf   Ⓒ earmuffs   Ⓓ boots   Ⓔ sweater

7   **hammer**   **wrench**   **screwdriver**

Ⓐ nail   Ⓑ saw   Ⓒ paper   Ⓓ glue   Ⓔ coin

8   **earthquake**   **drought**   **tornado**

A clouds   B mist   C hurricane   D waves   E wreck

9   **snow**   **polar bear**   **teeth**

A tongue   B glasses   C juice   D lemon   E cotton

10   **Monday**   **Tuesday**   **Wednesday**

A Friday   B week   C Saturday   D April   E day

11   **stream**   **bay**   **pond**

A dam   B ditch   C aquarium   D sea   E fountain

12   **orange**   **green**   **purple**

A red   B yellow   C color   D blue   E pink

13   **inch**   **foot**   **yard**

(A) pound   (B) mile   (C) gram   (D) length   (E) quart

14   **dawn**   **start**   **launch**

(A) begin   (B) trip   (C) day   (D) end   (E) voyage

15   **pyramid**   **prism**   **sphere**

(A) angle   (B) circle   (C) triangle   (D) base   (E) cube

16   **play**   **recital**   **concert**

(A) stage   (B) seat   (C) music   (D) museum   (E) opera

17   **trio**   **third**   **triplet**

(A) double   (B) square   (C) triangle   (D) rectangle   (E) twin

18　　**violinist**　　　　**guitarist**　　　　**trumpeter**

　　　A　musician　　　B　composer　　　C　conductor　　　D　drummer　　　E　band

19　　**orbit**　　　　**rotate**　　　　**revolve**

　　　A　move　　　B　planet　　　C　spin　　　D　bounce　　　E　shift

20　　**route**　　　　**highway**　　　　**lane**

　　　A　parking lot　　　B　freeway　　　C　field　　　D　car　　　E　map

21　　**Canada**　　　　**France**　　　　**Brazil**

　　　A　India　　　B　Asia　　　C　North America　　　D　Pacific　　　E　California

SENTENCE COMPLETION

Maya

Directions (Read these aloud to your child.):

In each question, there is a missing word. First, read the sentence. Then, look below the sentence at each of the answer choices. Which choice would go best in the sentence?

Additional information (for parents): Page 10 provides Sentence Completion tips.

1   **Dad had to _____ the ladder carefully to reach the kitten stuck up in the tree.**

A drop   B climb   C twist   D lower   E go down

2   **Because of the thunderstorm, we _____ our field trip at the outdoor amusement park.**

A planned   B toured   C saw   D canceled   E continued

3   **The slowest horse will _____ the contest.**

A see   B win   C begin   D view   E lose

4   **Our class plans to _____ a mural to decorate the hallway.**

A erase   B ignore   C create   D wash   E clean

5 The kitten was so _____ that it fell asleep in my lap five minutes after we got home.

A sleepy   B awake   C strong   D curious   E fierce

6 Old photos help us to _____ life 100 years ago.

A forget   B bury   C hide   D imagine   E photograph

7 My little brother is very _____ about trying new foods and usually says no right away.

A cheerful   B interested   C picky   D excited   E brave

8 The lifeguard blew the whistle, _____ the swimmers that it was time to leave the pool.

A thanking   B inviting   C teaching   D stopping   E warning

9 They put the injured bird in a box with a blanket to keep it safe and _____ until help arrived.

A frightened   B flying   C hungry   D warm   E cool

10 During the spelling bee, Mia had to _____ each word before saying her answer.

A repeat   B skip   C define   D whisper   E alphabetize

11 Even though he was tired, James _____ to finish his project before bedtime.

A refused   B managed   C disagreed   D complained   E avoided

12 The hikers walked on the narrow _____ through the forest to get to the waterfall.

A lake   B bay   C path   D crack   E hole

13 Acorns _____ on oak trees.

A drop   B bloom   C collect   D crack   E grow

14 The magician used a clever trick to _____ the audience during the show.

A bore   B disappoint   C entertain   D upset   E delay

15   **They feared the strong wave would _____ the sandcastle.**

    ^A destroy   ^B help   ^C support   ^D strengthen   ^E melt

16   **The teacher used a calm voice to _____ the upset student.**

    ^A challenge   ^B startle   ^C ignore   ^D comfort   ^E forget

17   **If you leave the windows open, the cold air from outside will _____ the temperature inside the house.**

    ^A raise   ^B measure   ^C prevent   ^D help   ^E lower

18   **Cleaning the large, dusty attic was a long and _____ task.**

    ^A joyful   ^B creative   ^C difficult   ^D secret   ^E lucky

19   **Pilots must stay _____ while flying the airplane.**

    ^A happy   ^B alert   ^C friendly   ^D floating   ^E moving

20 She had to _____ the song she practiced because there wasn't enough time left to perform the whole thing.

Ⓐ lengthen   Ⓑ learn   Ⓒ expand   Ⓓ shorten   Ⓔ listen to

Zoe

FIGURE ANALOGIES

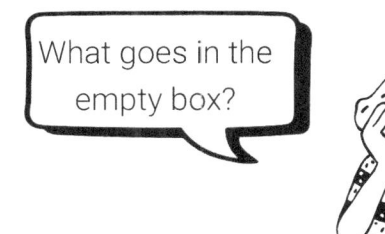

Sara

Directions: The pictures in the top boxes go together in some way. Look at the bottom boxes. One box is empty. Look at the row of pictures next to the boxes. These are the answer choices. Which one of these choices goes with the picture in the bottom box like the pictures in the top boxes go together?

Explanation (for parents): A more detailed explanation and a Figure Analogies example question is on p.10. Try to define a "rule" to describe how the top set belongs together. With Figure Analogies, this "rule" could describe a "change" that occurs from the top left box to the top right box. Next, take this "rule" describing the change, and apply it to the bottom picture.

Example: In the first shape group, we see a star, a pentagon, and a star. In the second group, we see the same shape group, but something has changed. Let's come up with a "rule" to describe this change. The top shape and middle shape switch their order.

Let's look in the bottom box. We see another shape group. It is a pentagon, a heart, and then a pentagon. Which answer choice follows our rule of the top shape and middle shape switching order? Look carefully at each answer choice. It is choice D. The first order was: pentagon, heart, pentagon. The order of choice D is heart, pentagon, pentagon.

1

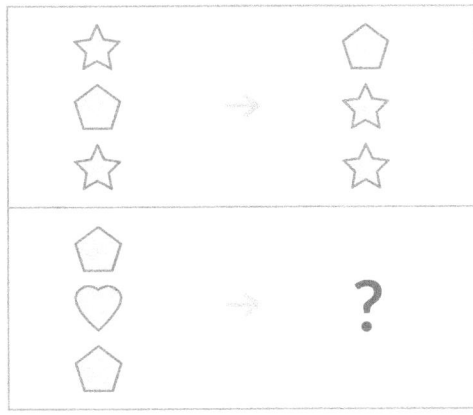    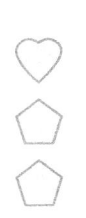 

A   B   C   D   E

2

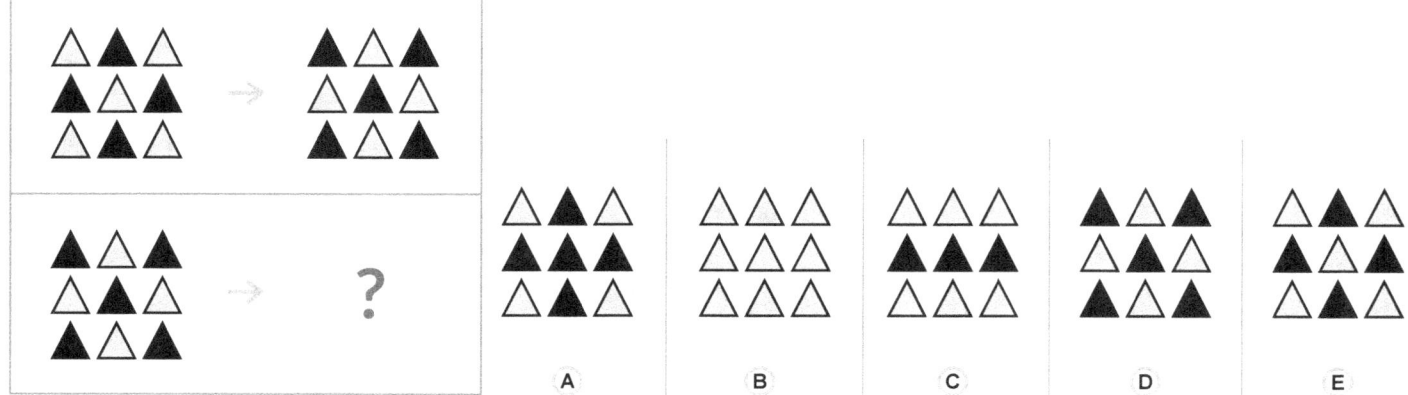

3

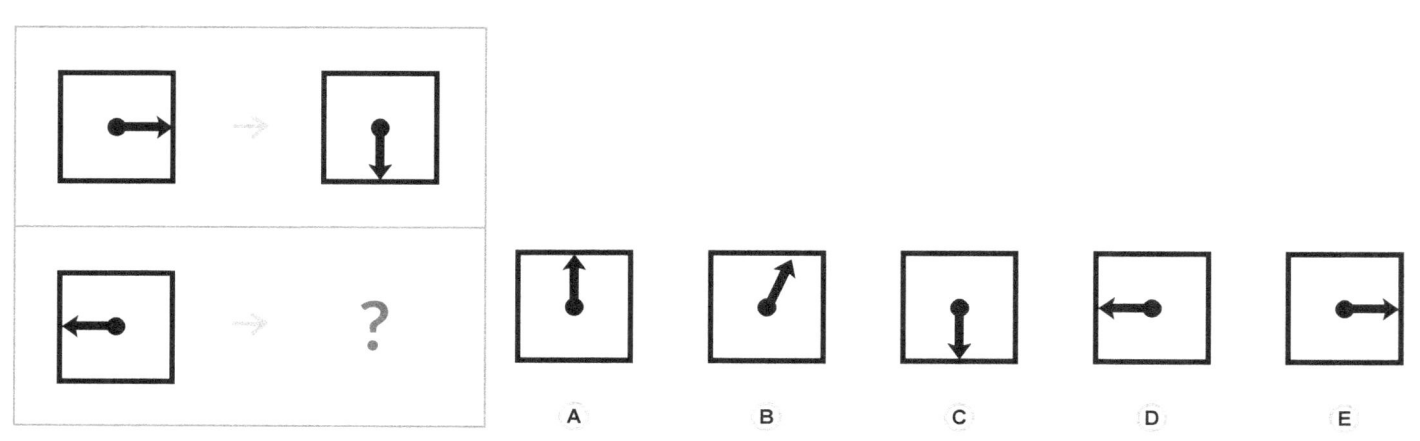

4

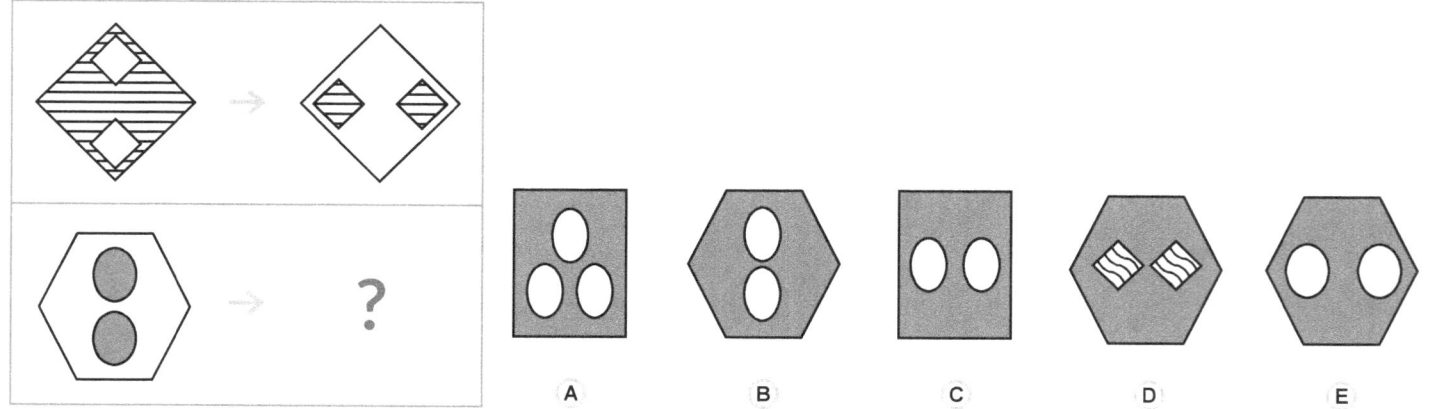

5

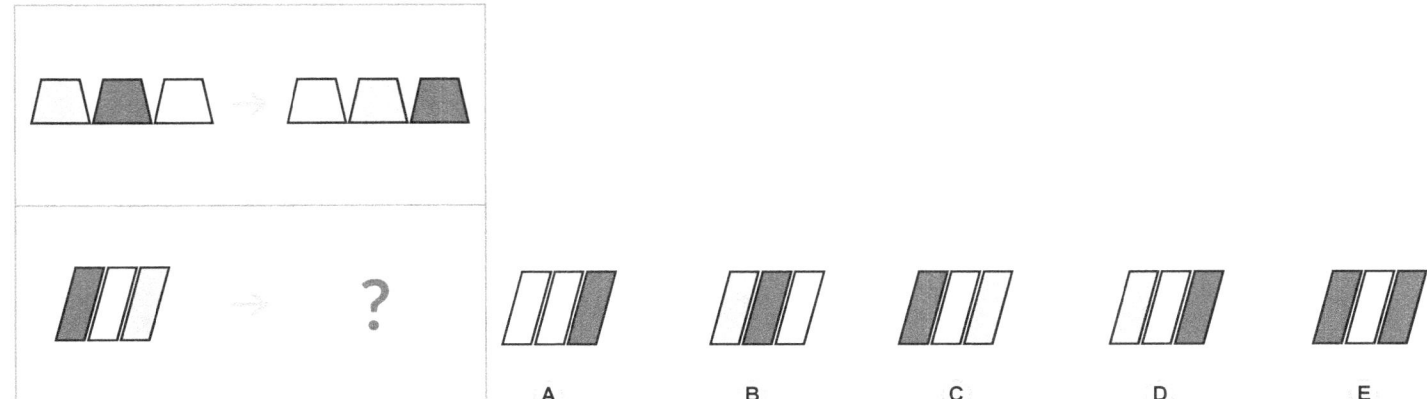

A   B   C   D   E

6

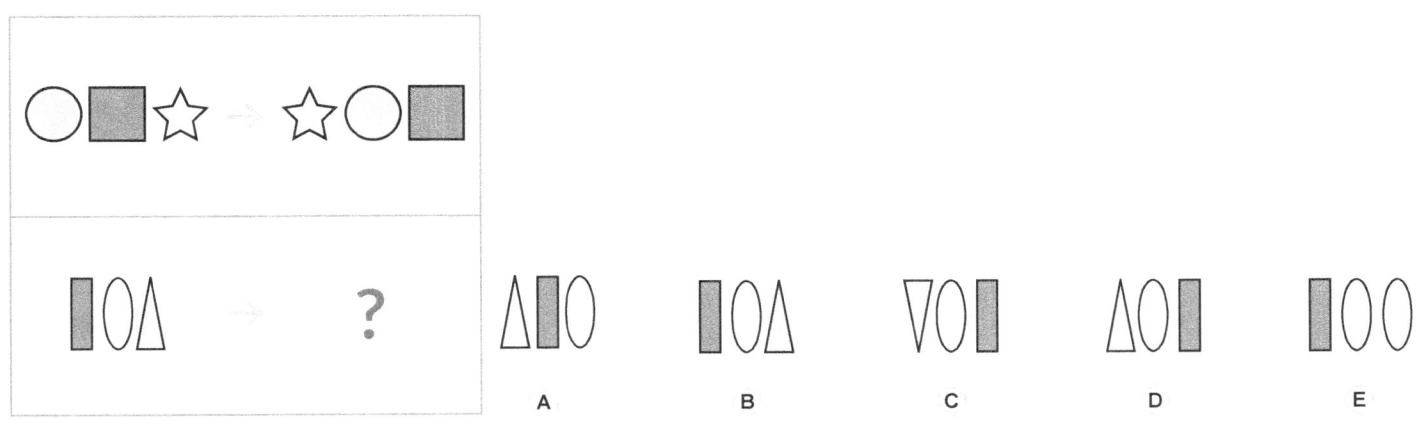

A   B   C   D   E

7

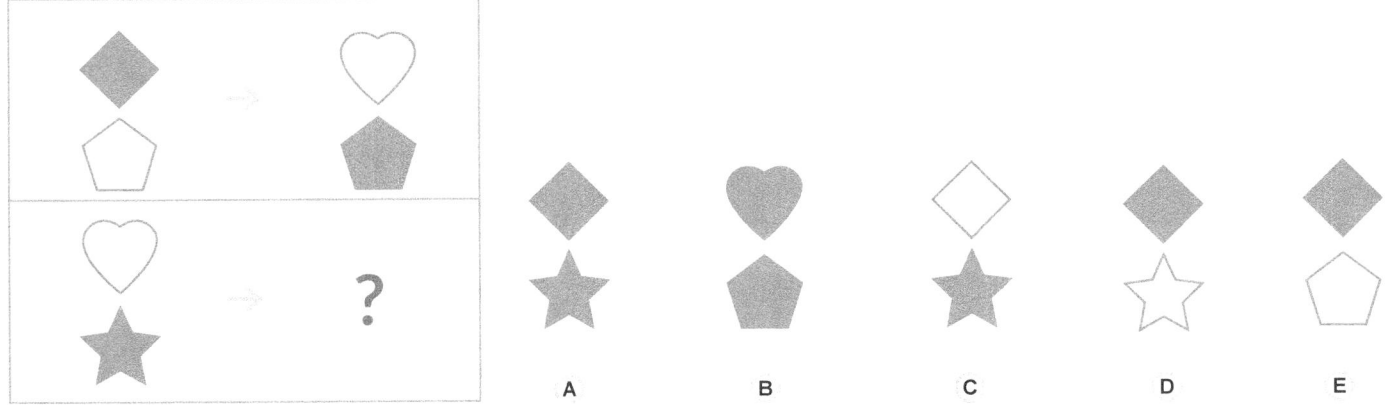

A   B   C   D   E

8

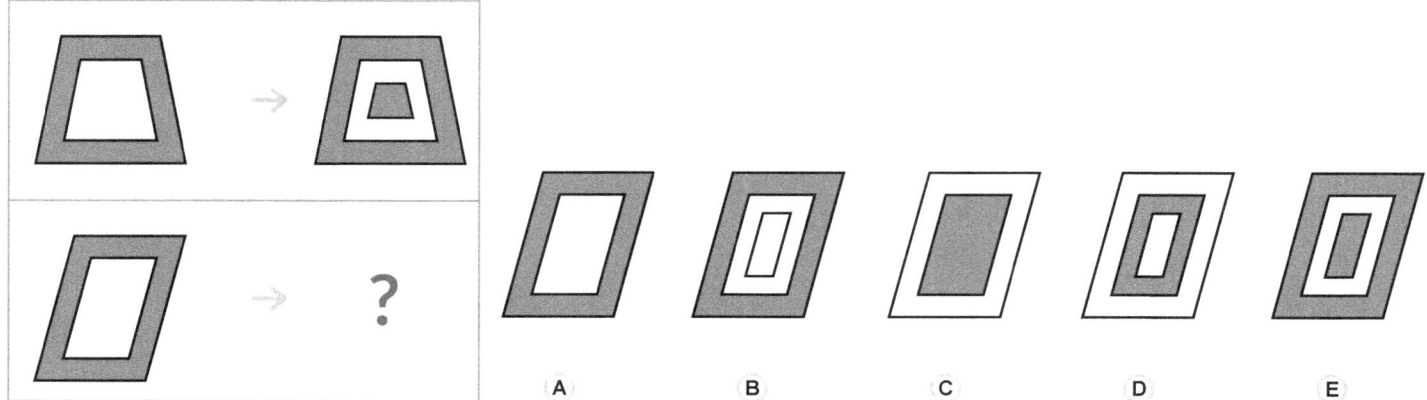

9

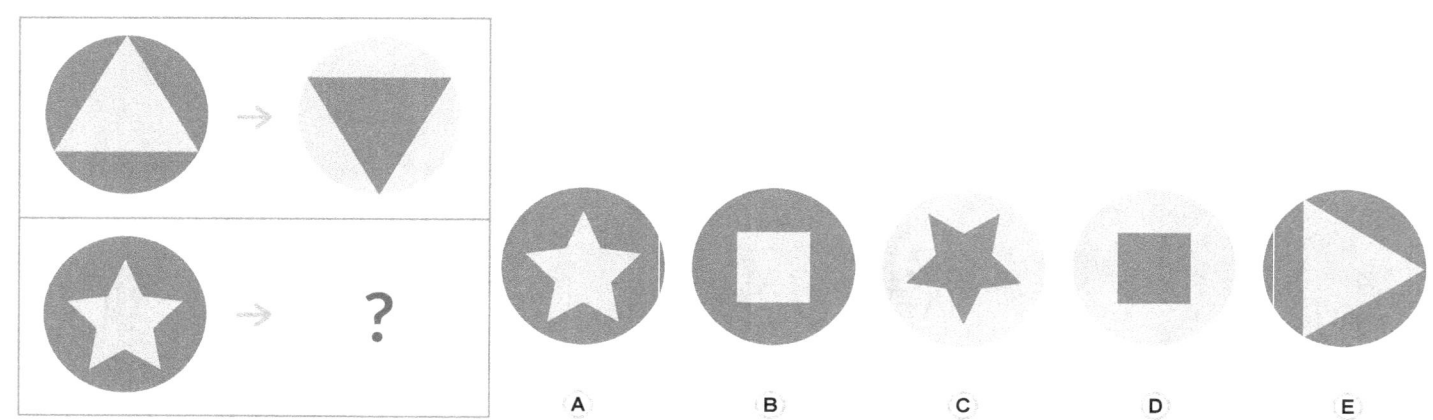

10

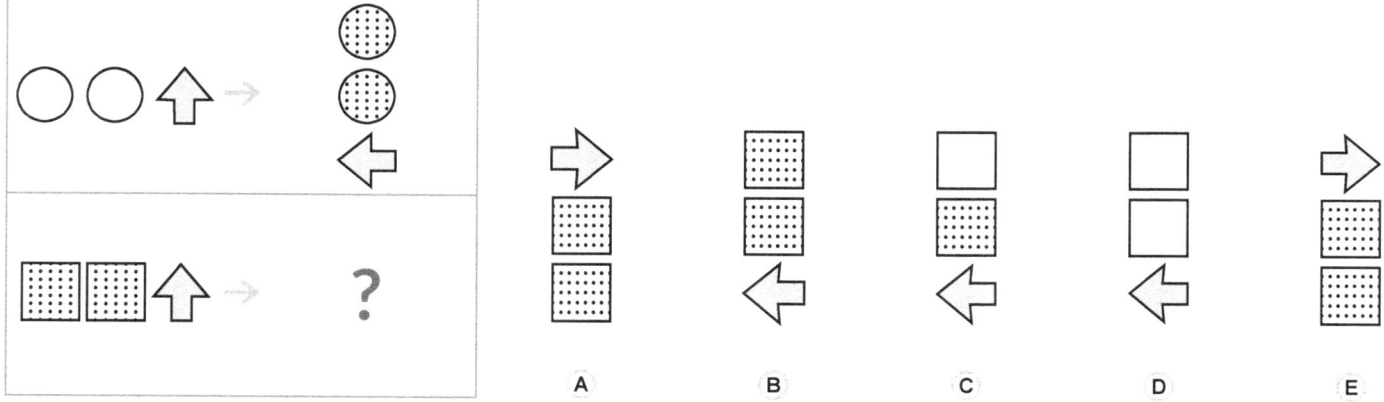

40

11

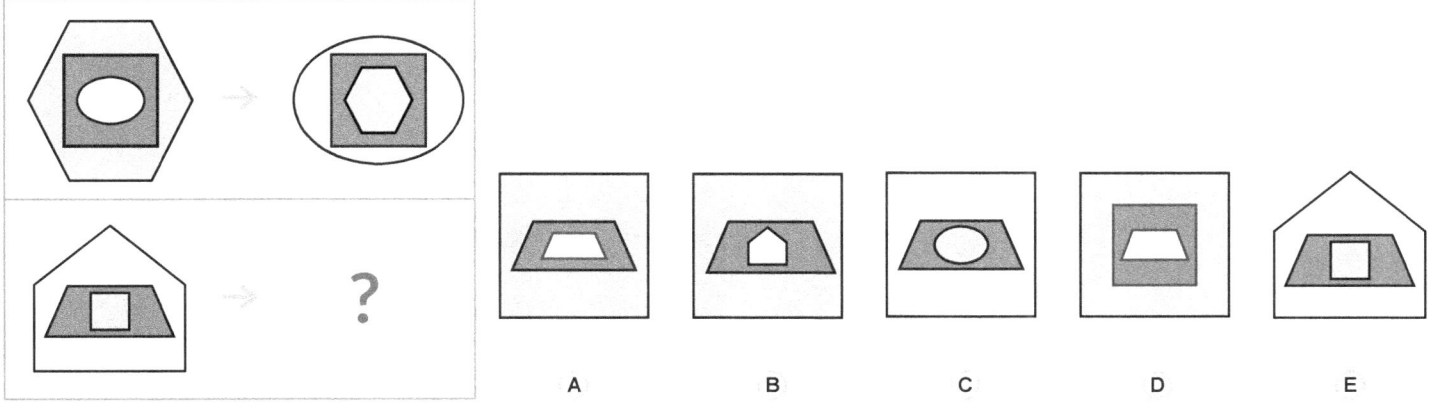

A B C D E

12

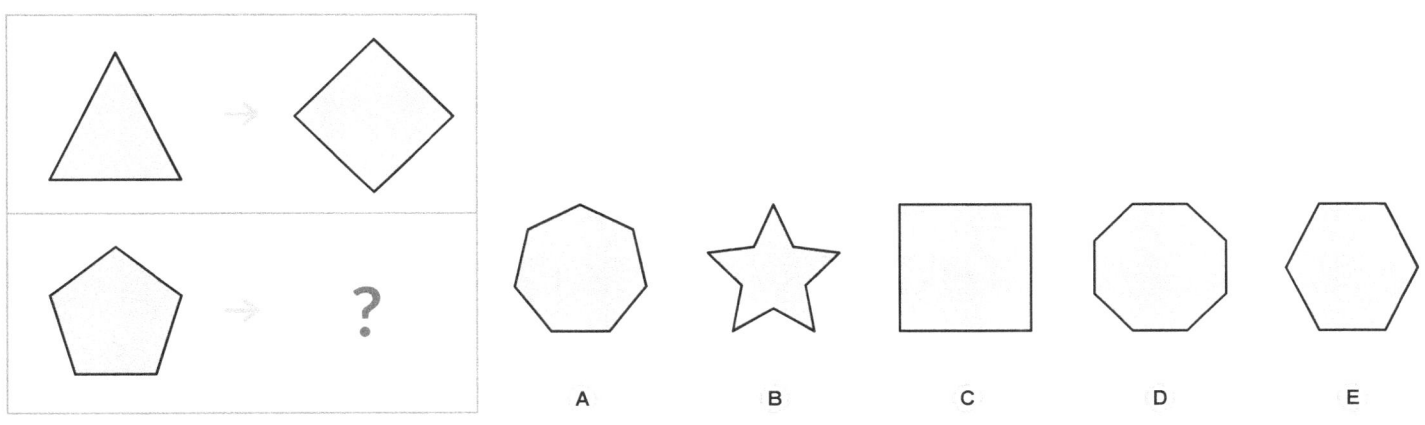

A B C D E

13

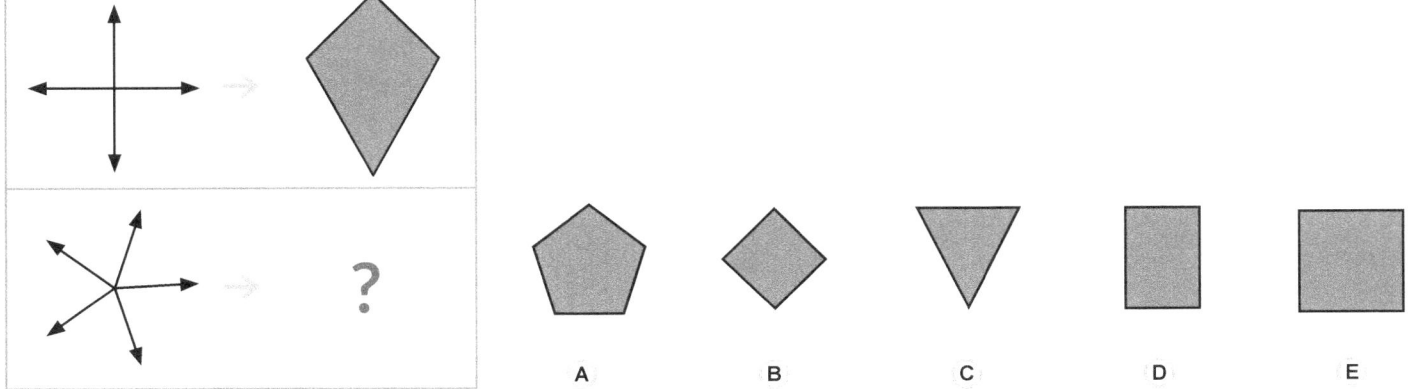

A B C D E

14

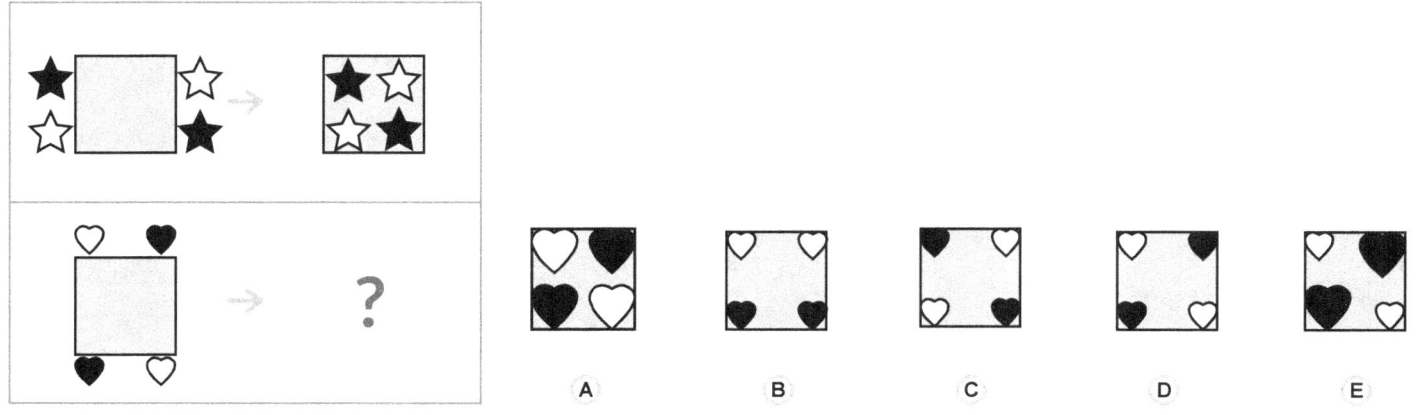

15

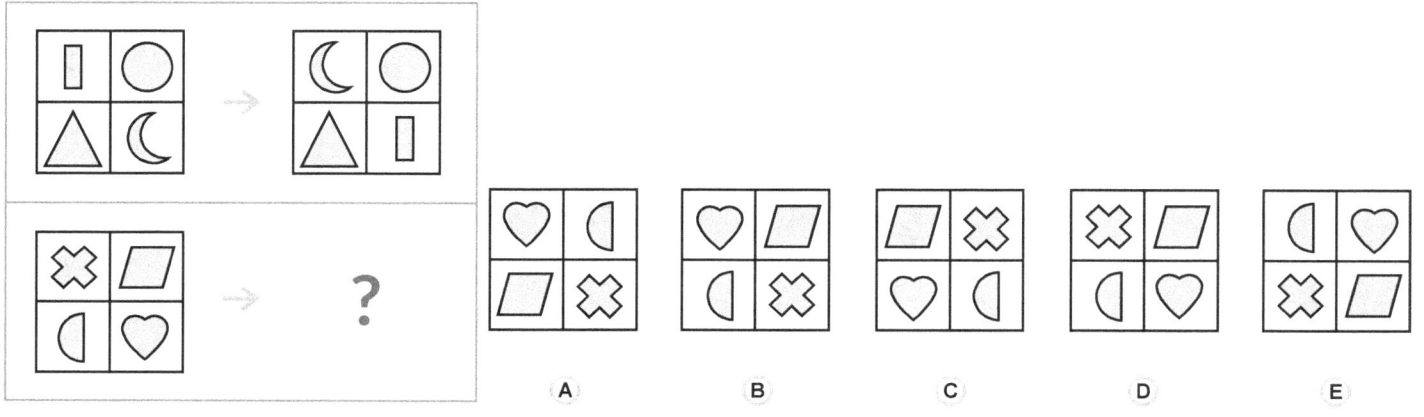

16

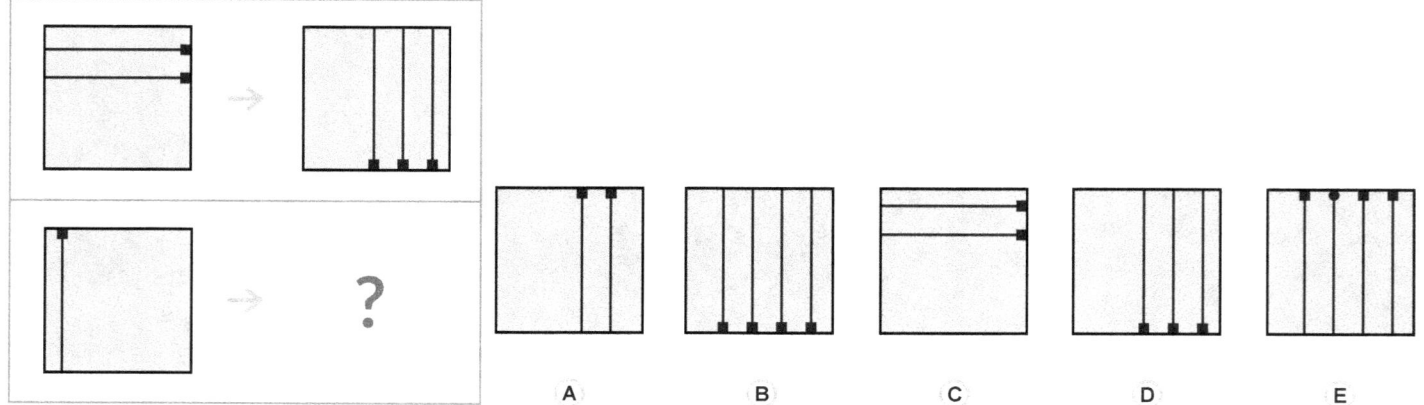

42

17

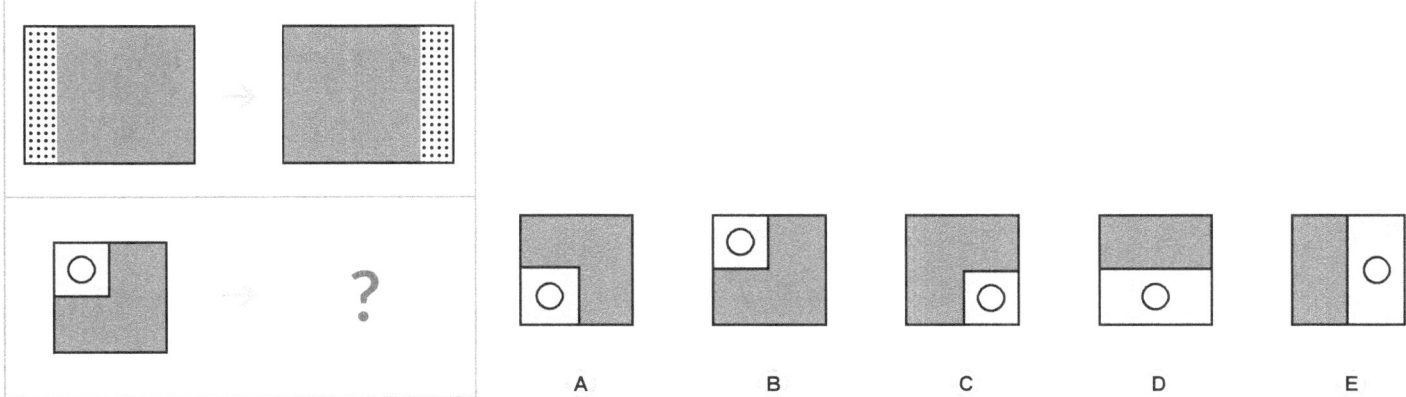

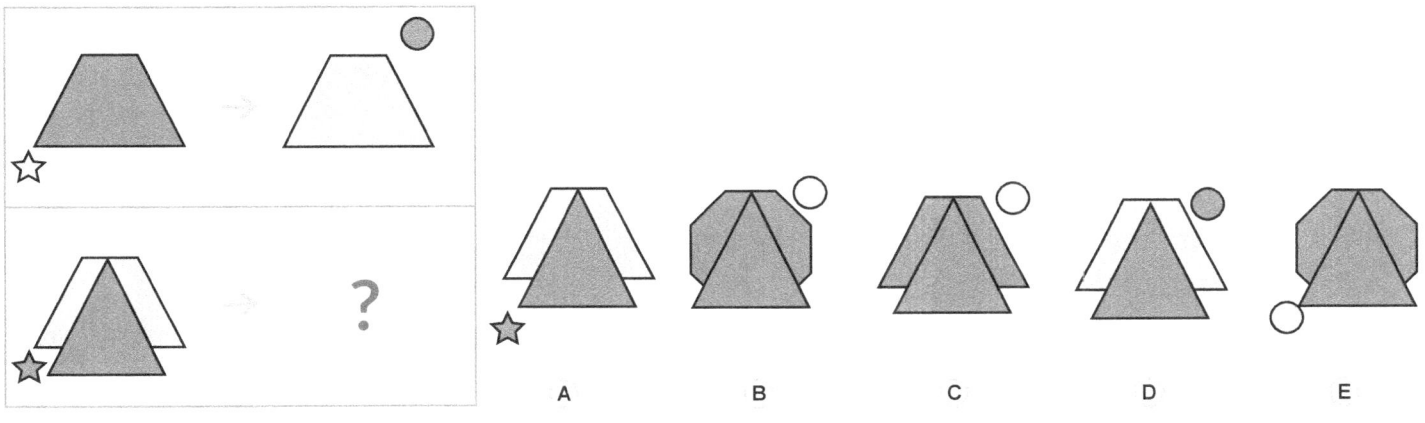

18

19

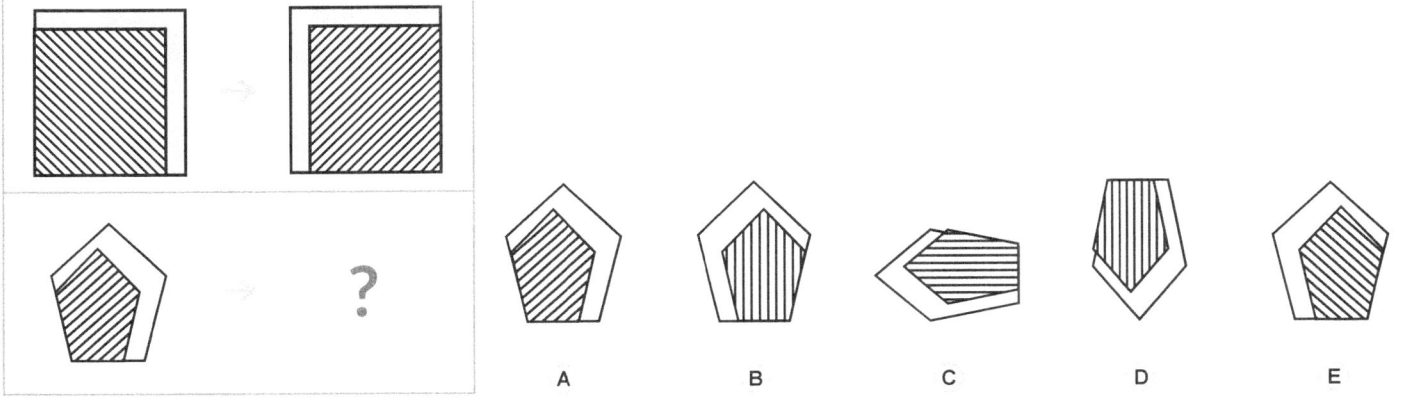

FIGURE CLASSIFICATION

What picture on the bottom goes best with those on top?

Kai

Directions: The top row shows three pictures that are alike in some way. Look at the bottom row. There are five pictures. Which picture in the bottom row goes best with the pictures in the top row?

Explanation (for parents): A more detailed explanation of Figure Classification questions is on p.12. Following is an excerpt.

Together with your child, try to figure out a "rule" describing how the top pictures are alike and belong together. Then, apply the "rule" to each answer choice to determine which one follows it.

If your child finds that more than one choice follows the rule, then a more specific rule is needed.

The "rule" for number 1 would be "the shape has vertical lines (lines that go up and down)." The shapes are different kinds of shapes - an oval, a parallelogram, and a pentagon. Also, on the bottom row, there are shapes that have different kinds of lines (horizontal lines going from left to right or dotted lines). However, there is only one choice that has vertical lines (lines going up and down). Choice A is the correct answer.

1

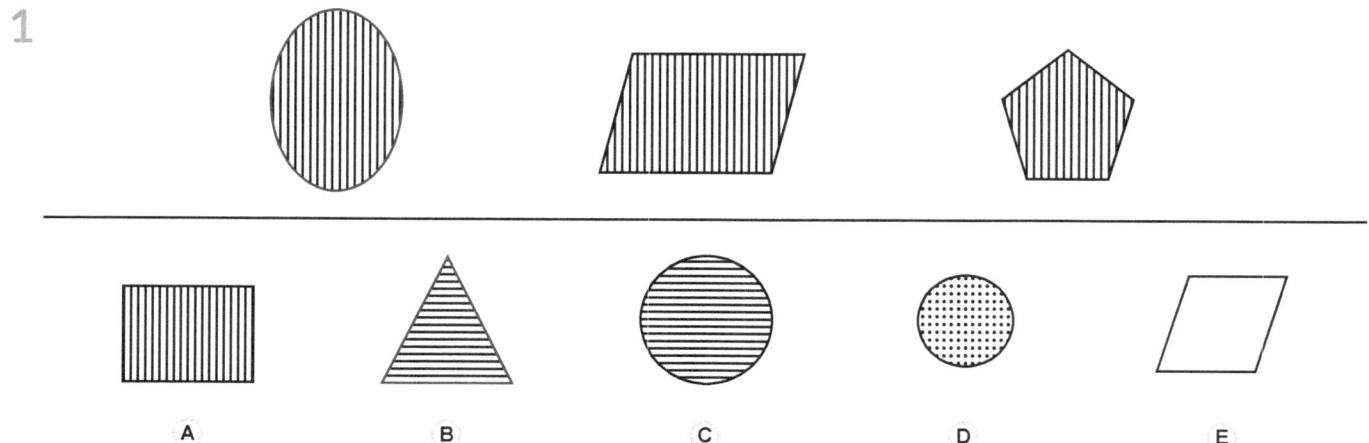

A   B   C   D   E

2

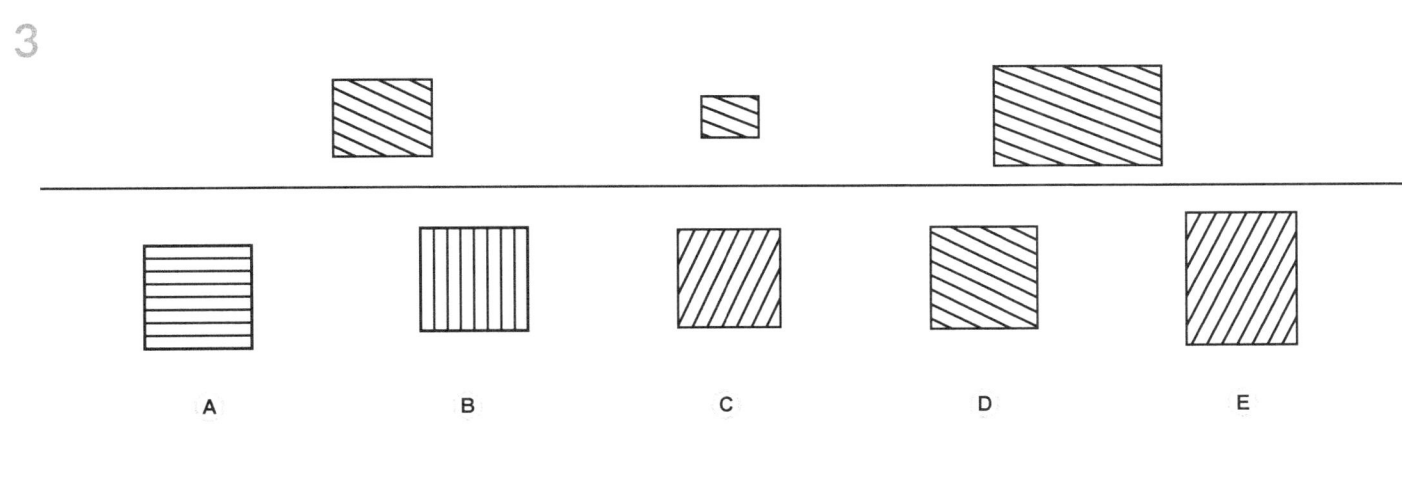

A   B   C   D   E

3

A   B   C   D   E

4

A   B   C   D   E

5

A   B   C   D   E

6

A   B   C   D   E

7

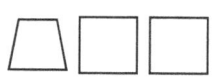  

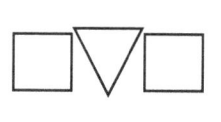 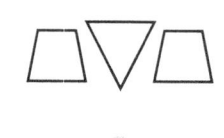 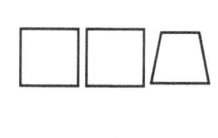 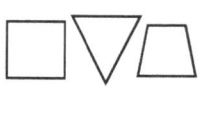

A   B   C   D   E

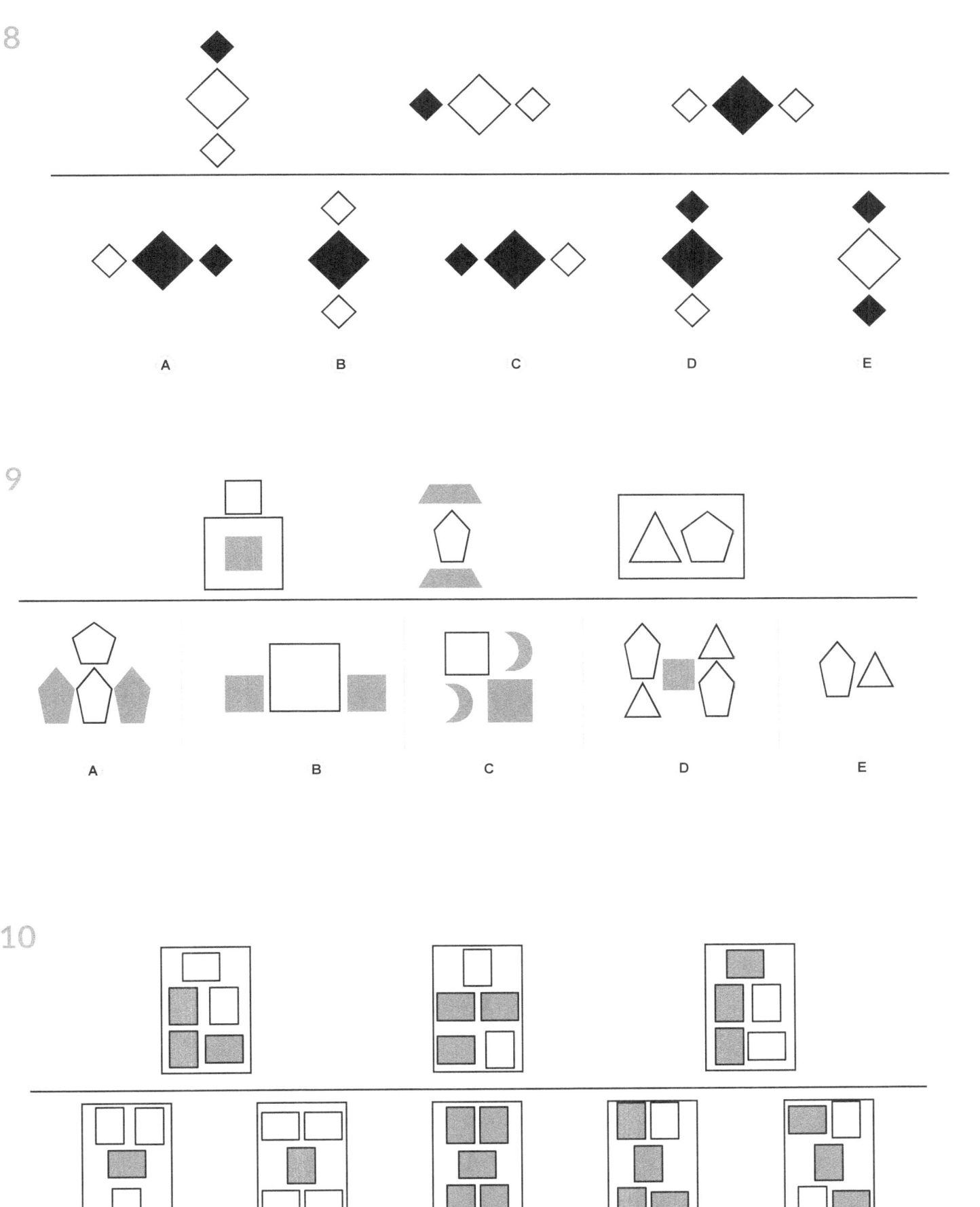

8

A B C D E

9

A B C D E

10

A B C D E

11

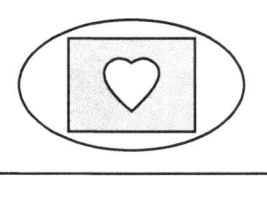  

 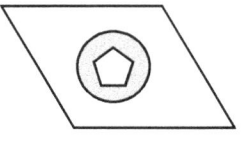  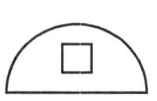

Ⓐ   Ⓑ   Ⓒ   Ⓓ   Ⓔ

12

 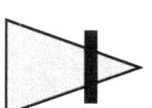 

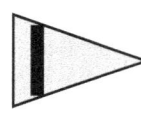  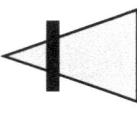 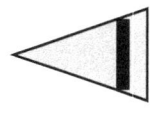

Ⓐ   Ⓑ   Ⓒ   Ⓓ   Ⓔ

13

  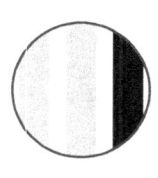 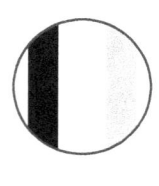 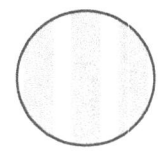

Ⓐ   Ⓑ   Ⓒ   Ⓓ   Ⓔ

14

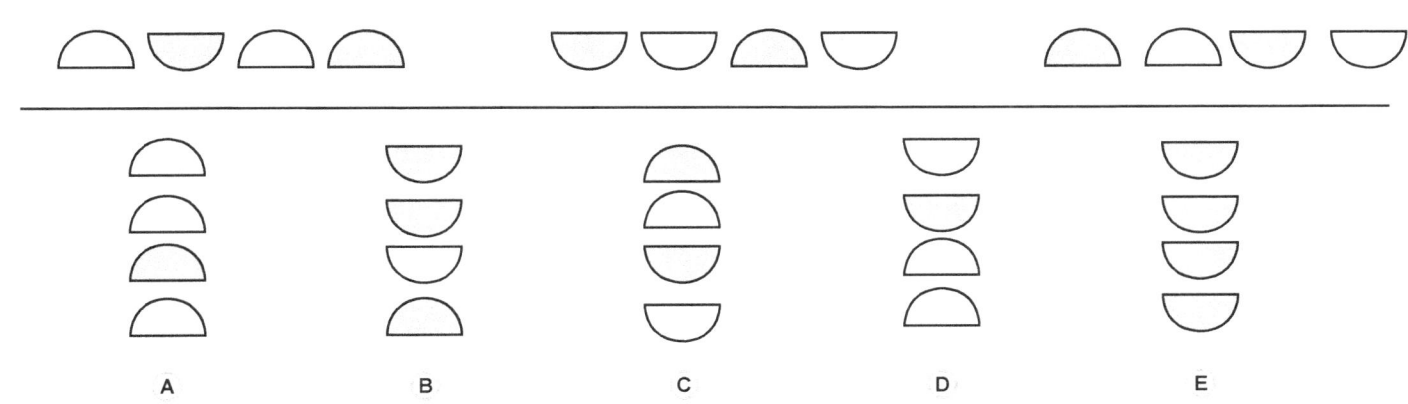

A   B   C   D   E

15

A   B   C   D   E

16

A   B   C   D   E

17

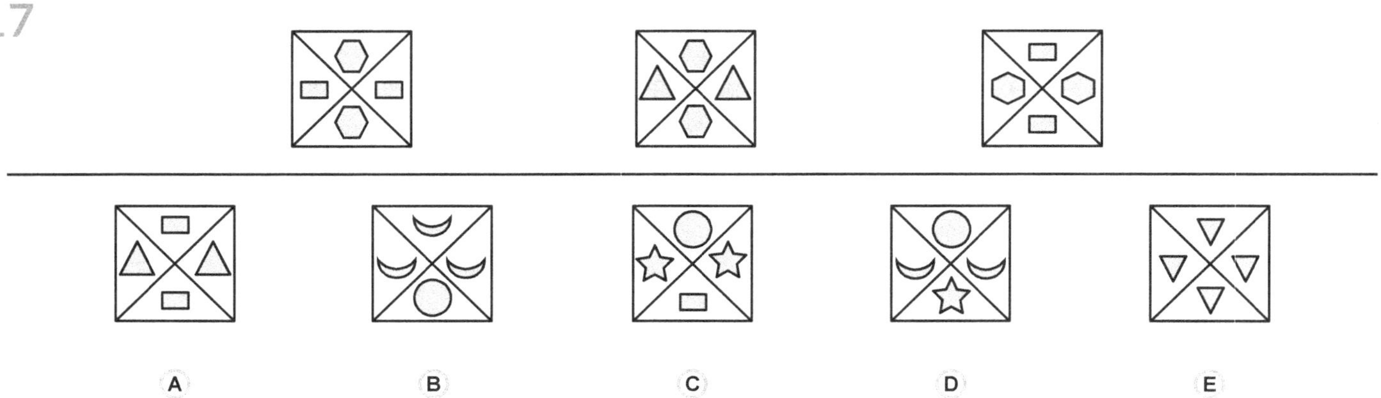

18

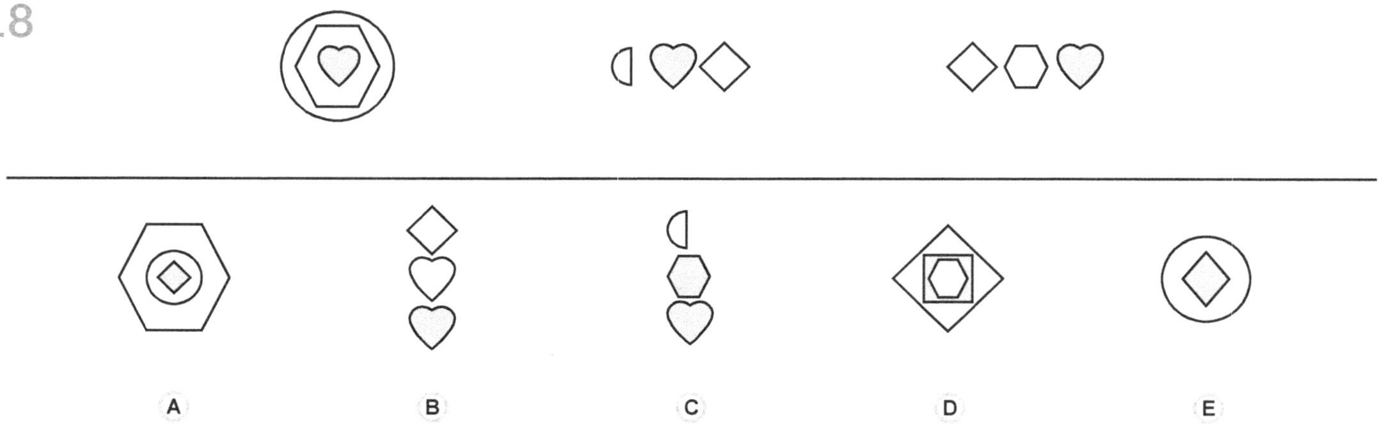

19

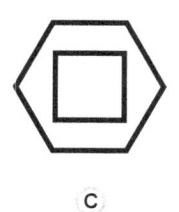

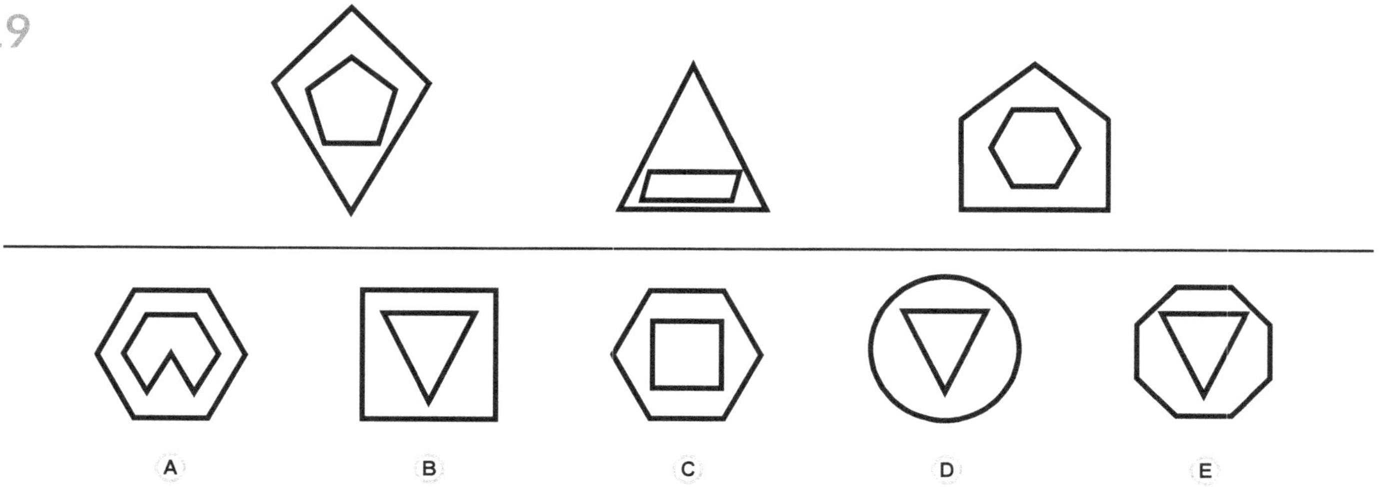

A B C D E

PAPER FOLDING

Look closely!

Maya

Directions: The top row of pictures shows a sheet of paper.
The paper was folded, then something was cut out. Which picture in the bottom row shows how the paper would look after it's unfolded?

Additional information (for parents): As explained earlier on p. 15, children may initially be "stumped" by Paper Folding. If your child needs help, then try demonstrating with real paper and a hole puncher.

Be sure to point out the number of holes made and their position after opening the paper.

1.

2.

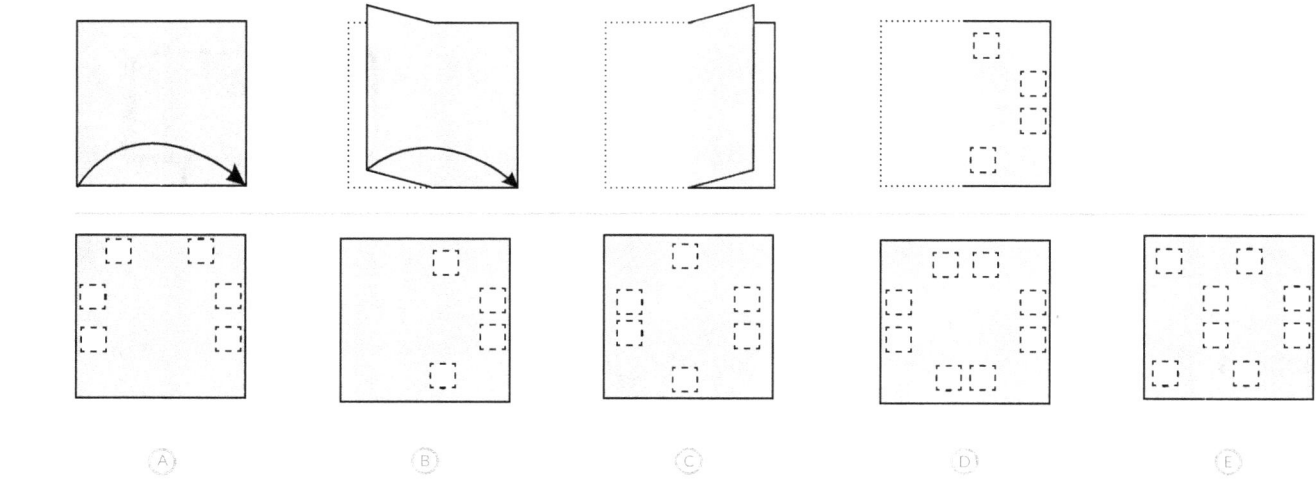

4.

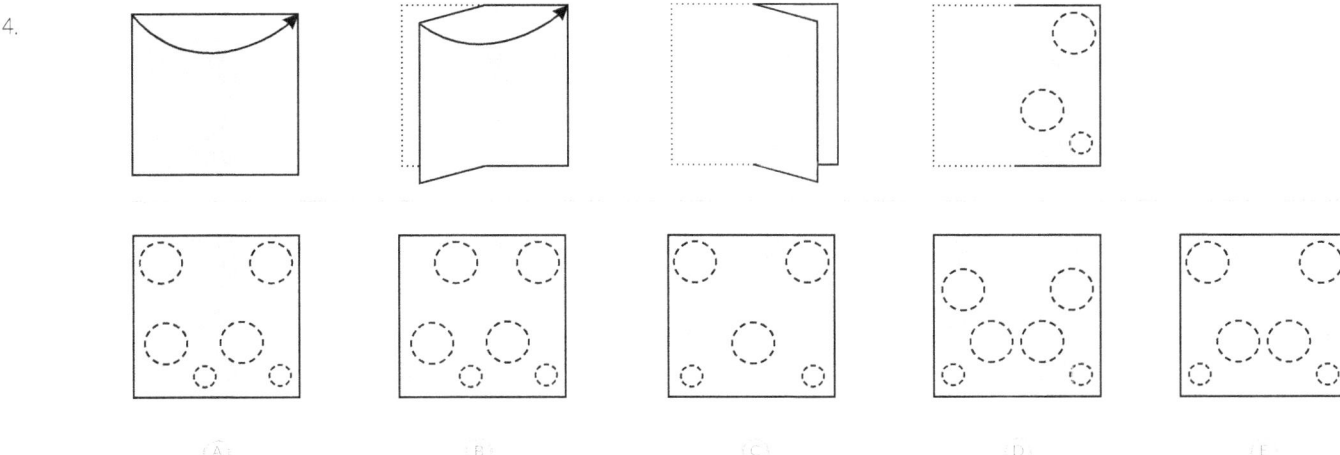

5.

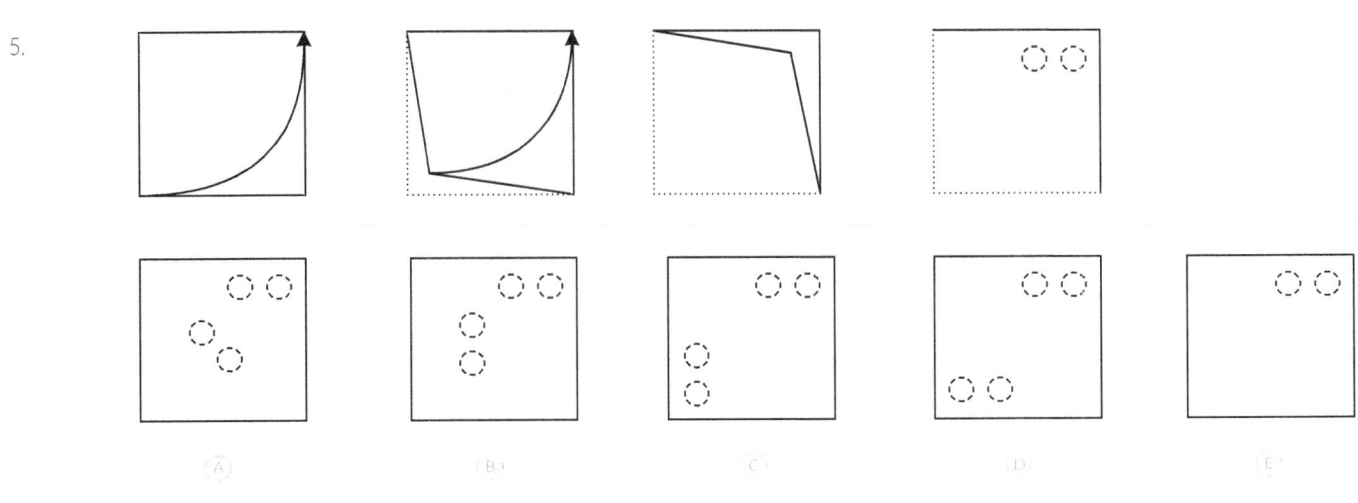

6.

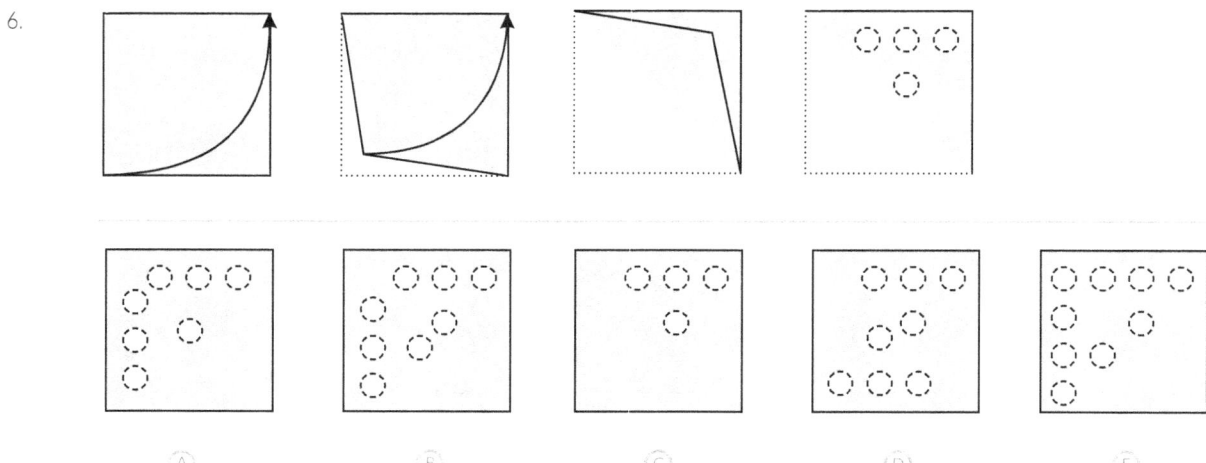

7.

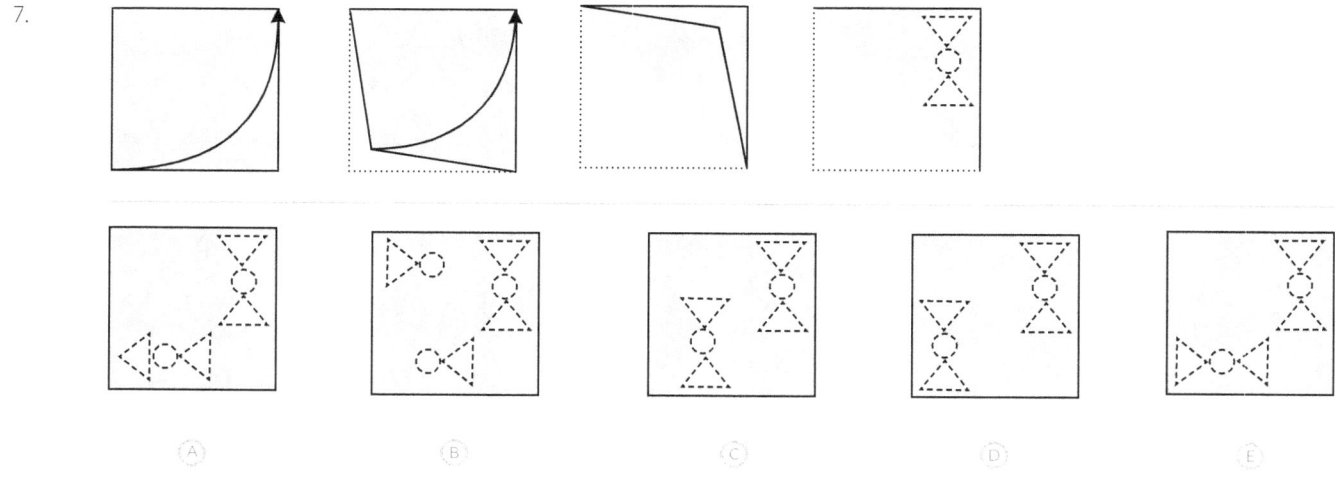

8.

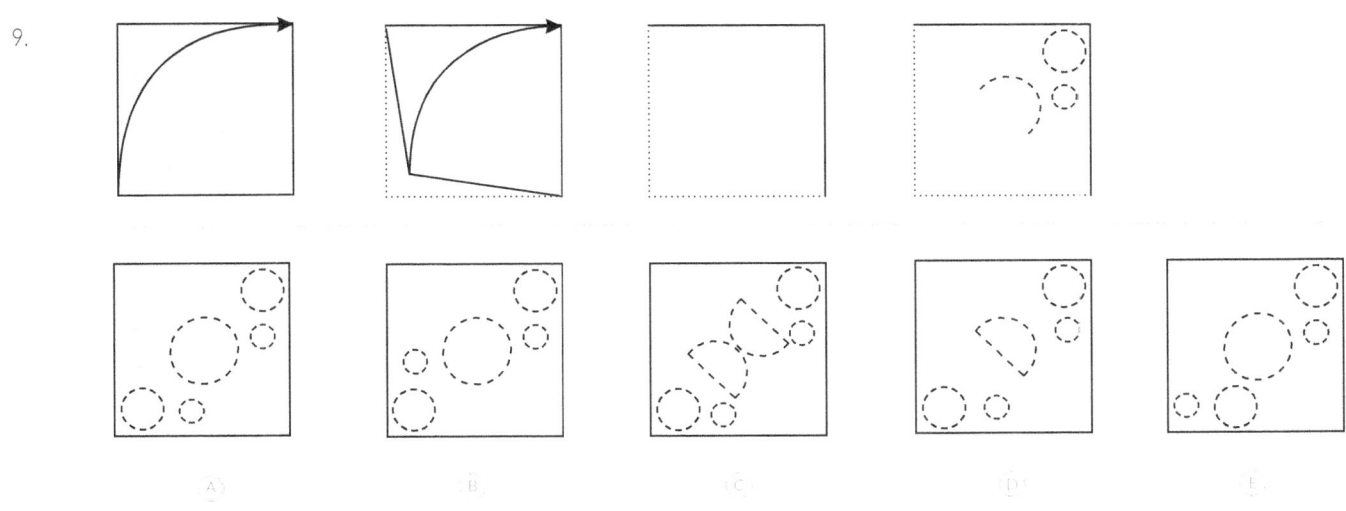

9.

Note: In the next questions, the paper is folded twice. Point this out to your child.

10.

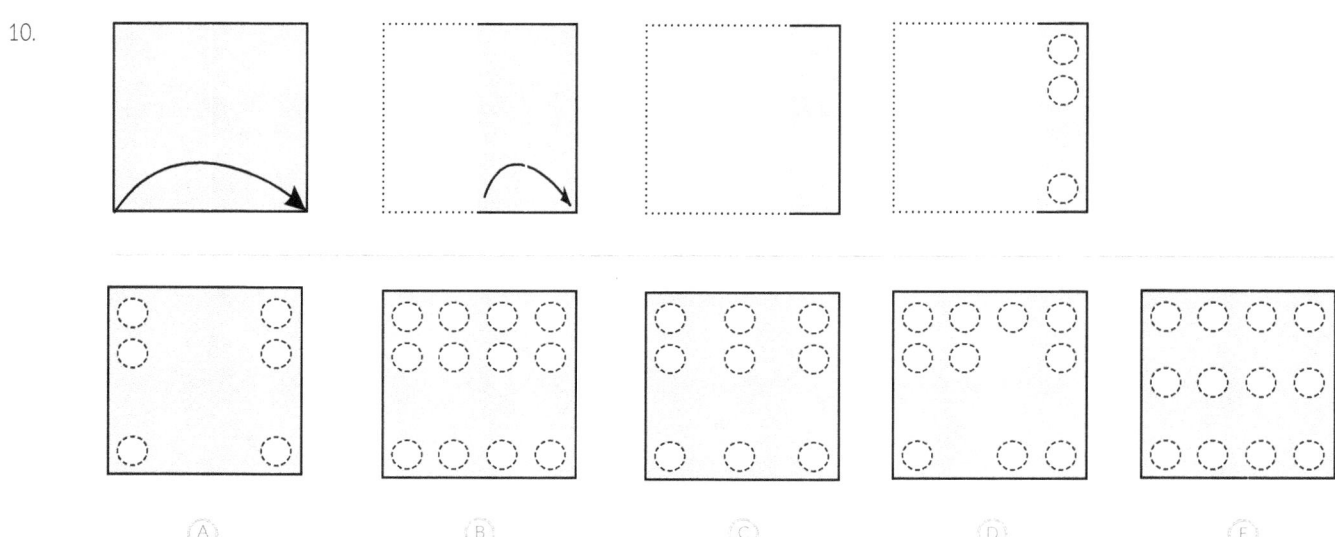

11.

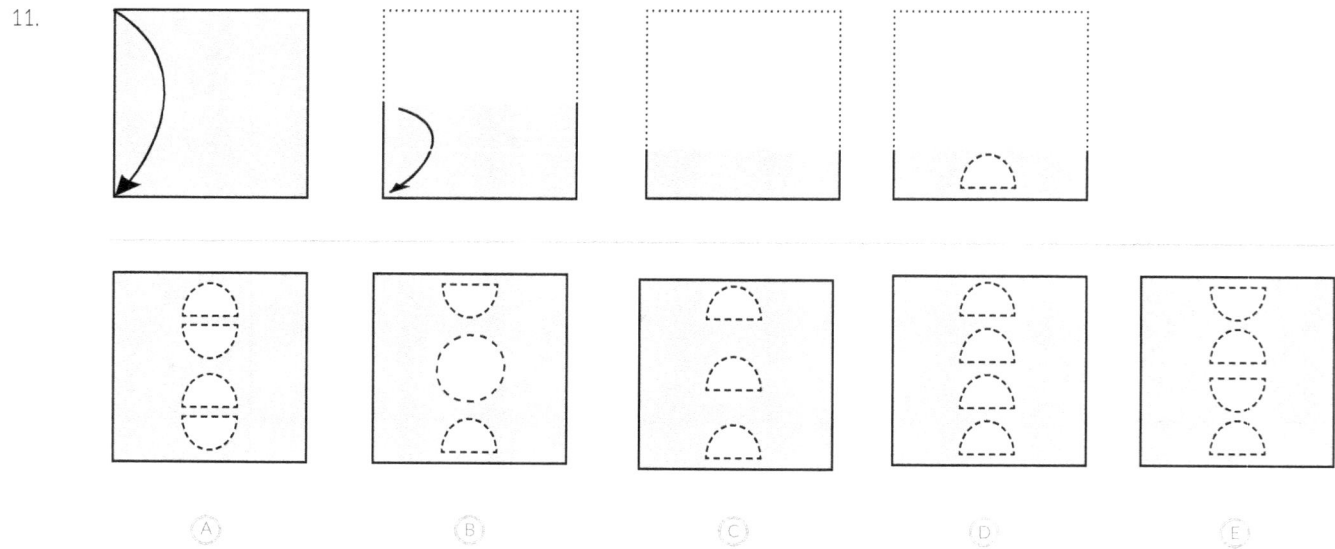

12.

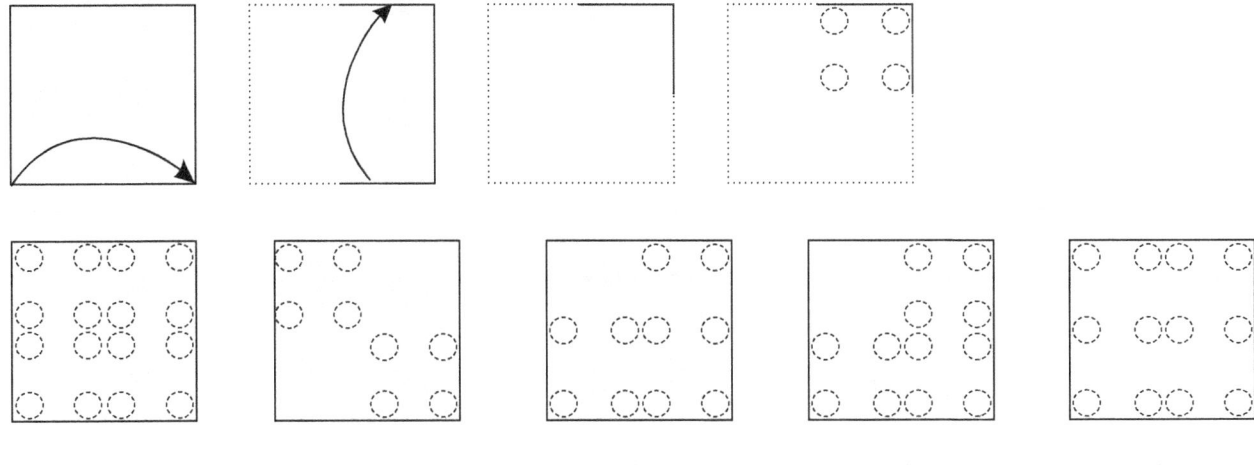

13.

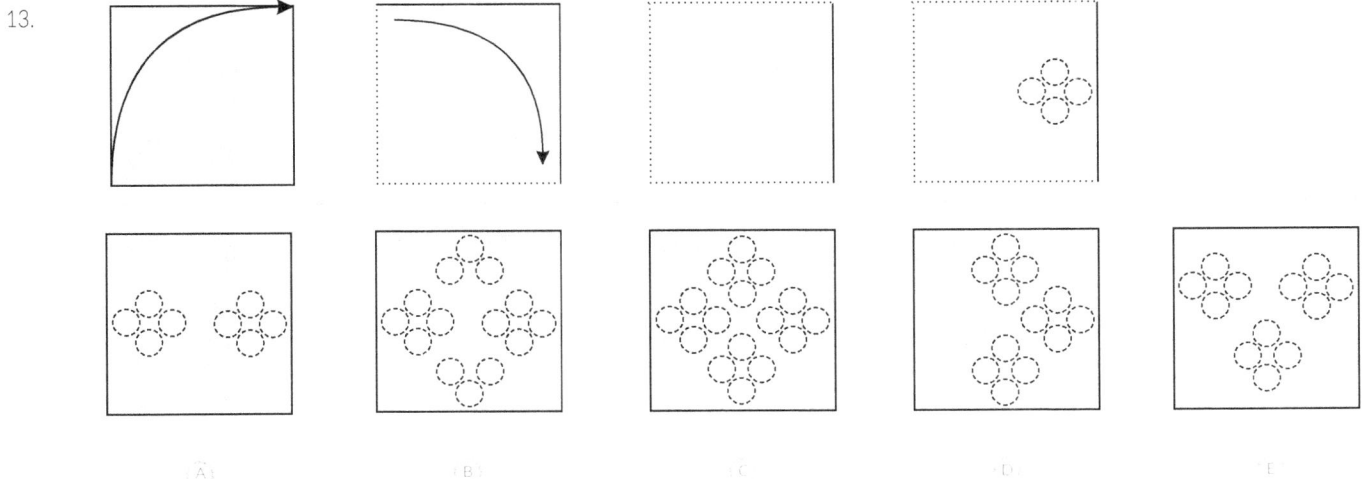

14.

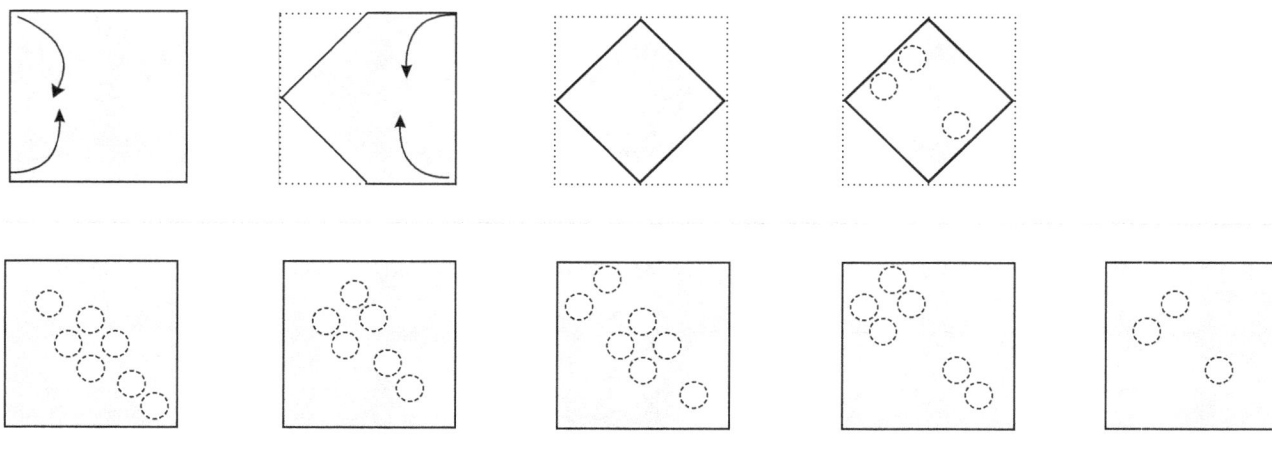

15.

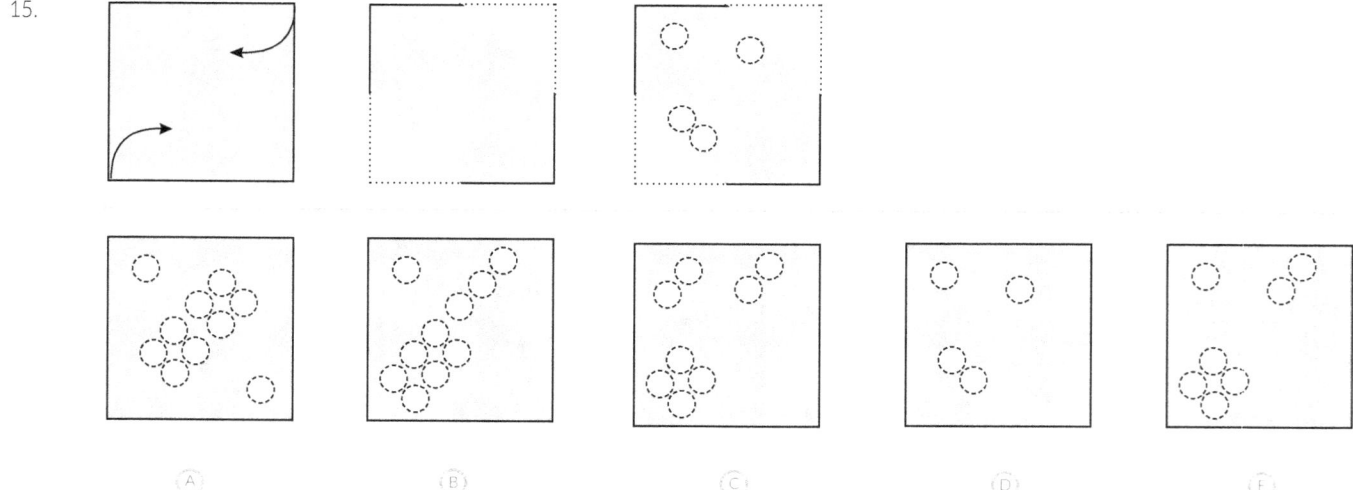

NUMBER PUZZLES

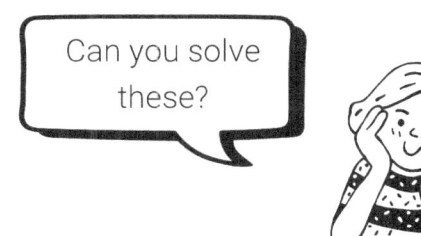

Can you solve these?

Sara

Directions (read to child): Look at the box that has the question mark. Which number would go here so that both of the sides of this equal sign (point to the equal sign) have the same amount?

Additional information (for parents): Be sure your child pays attention to the plus and minus signs. Some questions have two different signs. During the actual test, your child will most likely be able to use scratch paper. So, allow them to use scratch paper here if they wish. Page 17 has additional Number Puzzles tips.

Example: The left side of the equal sign has 14. Which answer choice do you need to put in place of the question mark so that the right side of the equal sign totals 14?

19 minus 5 equals 14. So, C is the correct answer. Be sure to choose C (5) and not B (14).

1   **14 = 19 – ❓**

A 3   B 14   C 5   D 6   E 4

2   **22 + 19 = 55 – ❓**

A 11   B 12   C 13   D 14   E 41

3   40   =   48   +   5   –   [?]

(A) 13   (B) 12   (C) 14   (D) 3   (E) 53

4   35   =   50   –   18   +   [?]

(A) 2   (B) 3   (C) 4   (D) 5   (E) 6

5   88   =   47   +   29   +   [?]

(A) 9   (B) 11   (C) 70   (D) 13   (E) 12

6   70   –   14   =   60   –   [?]

(A) 4   (B) 6   (C) 8   (D) 10   (E) 12

7   28   +   37   =   80   –   [?]

(A) 13   (B) 14   (C) 15   (D) 16   (E) 17

8 $78 = 63 - 5 + \boxed{?}$

A 17   B 10   C 19   D 20   E 21

Note: In the rest of the questions, your child will need to replace the black diamond with the given value to solve the problem.

9 $\boxed{?} = \blacklozenge + 55$
$\blacklozenge = 17$

A 70   B 71   C 72   D 73   E 74

10 $\boxed{?} = \blacklozenge \times 6$
$\blacklozenge = 7$

A 1   B 41   C 42   D 43   E 13

11 $\boxed{?} = \blacklozenge \div 2$
$\blacklozenge = 28$

A 12   B 14   C 15   D 16   E 26

12 $\boxed{?} = \blacklozenge \times 9$
$\blacklozenge = 4$

A 13   B 33   C 34   D 35   E 36

13

$$\boxed{?} = \blacklozenge \div 6$$
$$\blacklozenge = 36$$

Ⓐ 6   Ⓑ 5   Ⓒ 30   Ⓓ 7   Ⓔ 8

14

$$\boxed{?} = \blacklozenge + 22 - 14$$
$$\blacklozenge = 31$$

Ⓐ 38   Ⓑ 39   Ⓒ 40   Ⓓ 41   Ⓔ 5

15

$$\boxed{?} = \blacklozenge + 12 + 33$$
$$\blacklozenge = 10$$

Ⓐ 54   Ⓑ 55   Ⓒ 56   Ⓓ 57   Ⓔ 58

16

$$\boxed{?} = \blacklozenge - 19 - 11$$
$$\blacklozenge = 60$$

Ⓐ 90   Ⓑ 29   Ⓒ 30   Ⓓ 31   Ⓔ 32

17

$$\boxed{?} = \blacklozenge + 4 + 6$$
$$\blacklozenge = 9$$

Ⓐ 18   Ⓑ 40   Ⓒ 42   Ⓓ 19   Ⓔ 46

NUMBER SERIES

What goes in place of the missing rod?

Kai

Directions (read to child): Here, you must try to figure out a pattern that the numbers have made. Which answer choice would complete the pattern?

Parent note: Some questions are in the form of #1 (an abacus). Some are in the form of #8 (a series of numbers). Pages 17-19 have additional Number Series tips.

Example #1: Here is an abacus. The abacus rods have made a pattern: 0 beads, 9 beads, 0 beads, 7 beads, 0 beads, 5 beads, and 0 beads.

Here we see that every other rod has "0" beads. (The first, third, fifth, and seventh rods have 0.)

Also, every other rod (the second, fourth, and sixth rod) have two less beads each time.

If this is true, how many beads would the rod that is missing have? What is five take away two? It's 3.

So, the rod with 3 beads is the answer.

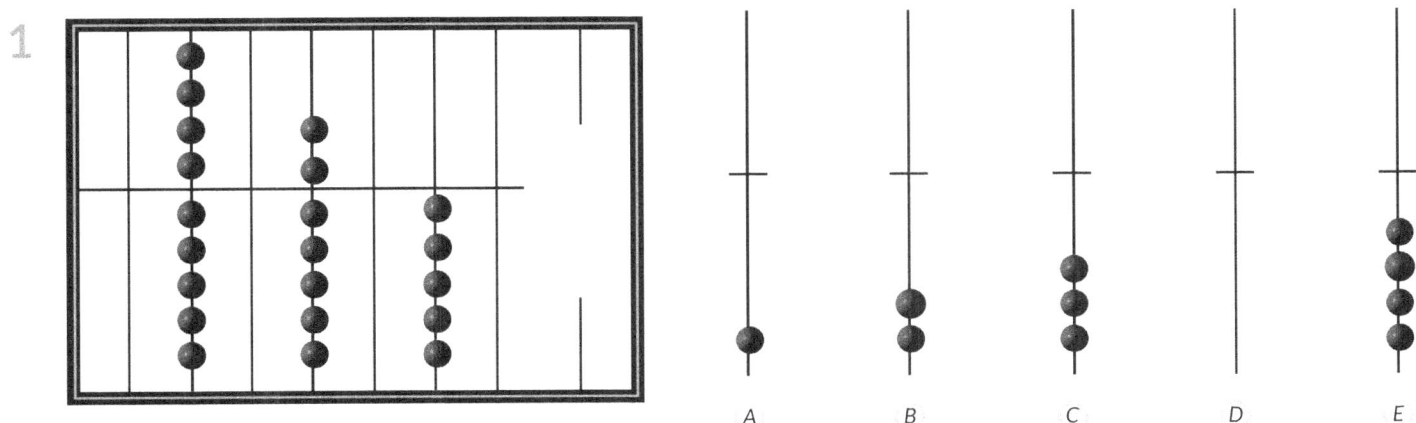

1

A   B   C   D   E

2

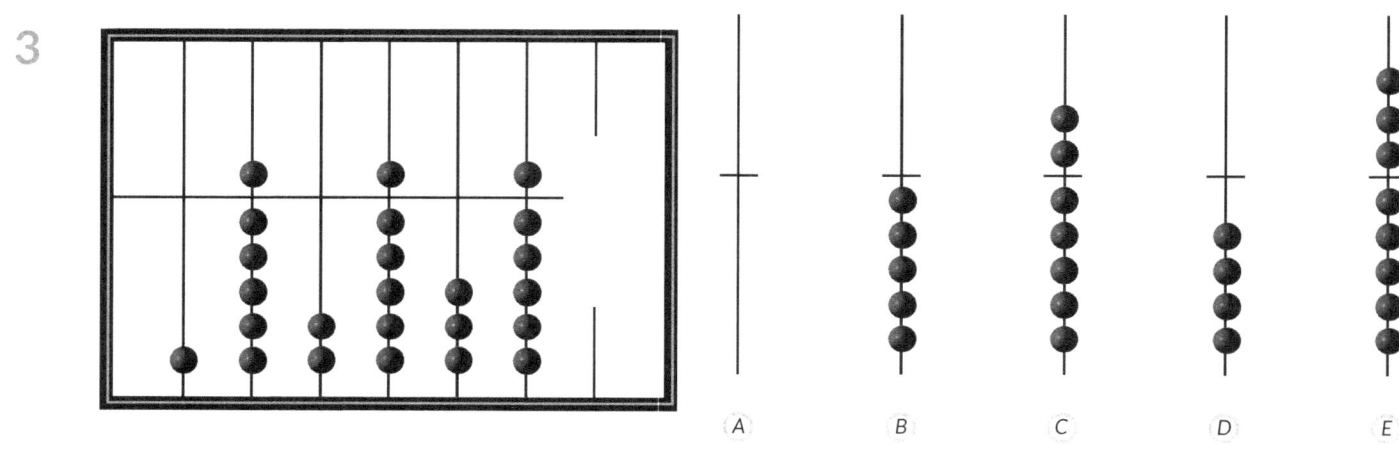

A B C D E

3

A B C D E

4

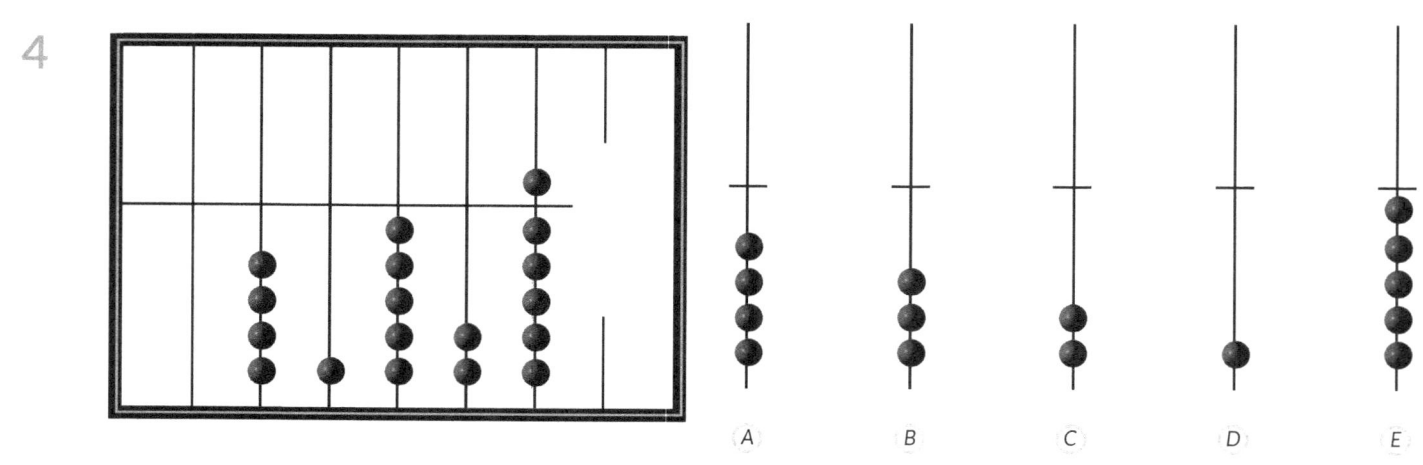

A B C D E

5

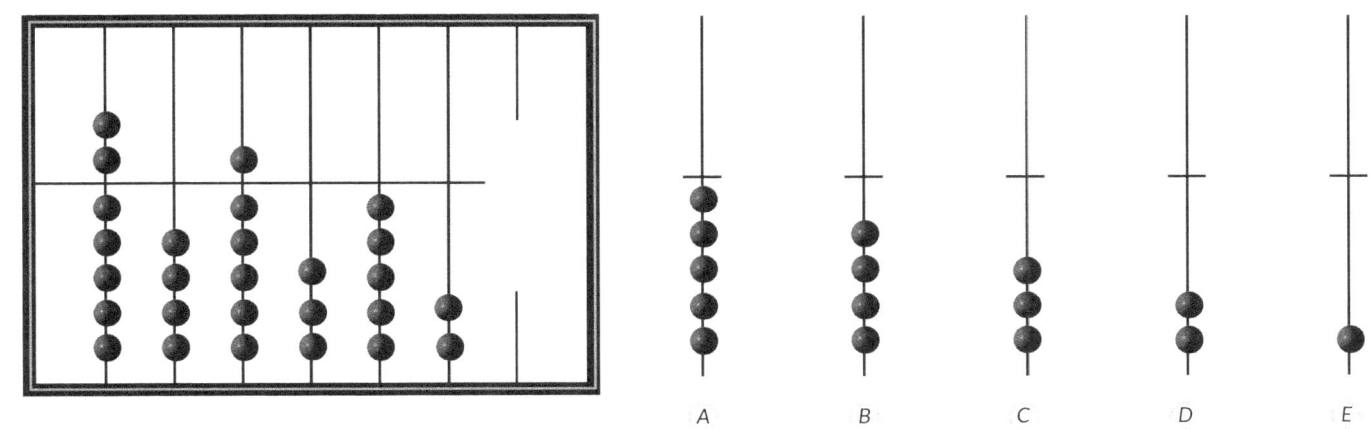

A   B   C   D   E

6

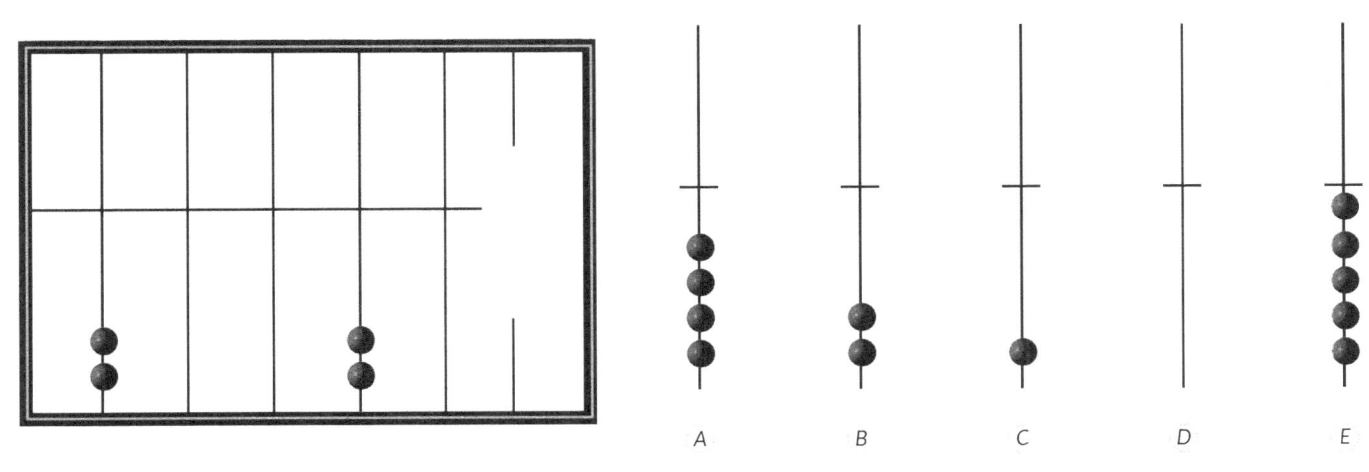

A   B   C   D   E

7

A   B   C   D   E

8.   **6**   **10**   **14**   **18**   **22**   **?**

(A) 24   (B) 25   (C) 26   (D) 27   (E) 28

9.   **2**   **3**   **5**   **6**   **8**   **9**   **?**

(A) 9   (B) 10   (C) 11   (D) 12   (E) 13

10.   **30**   **29**   **27**   **26**   **24**   **23**   **?**

(A) 21   (B) 22   (C) 20   (D) 19   (E) 18

11.   **4**   **6**   **9**   **11**   **14**   **16**   **?**

(A) 18   (B) 19   (C) 20   (D) 21   (E) 22

12.   **6**   **8**   **8**   **10**   **10**   **12**   **?**

(A) 16   (B) 13   (C) 14   (D) 15   (E) 12

13.   **18**   **17**   **16**   **14**   **13**   **12**   **10**   **?**

(A) 9   (B) 8   (C) 7   (D) 6   (E) 5

14   2.5   4.5   6.5   8.5   10.5   ?

   A 11   B 11.5   C 12.5   D 14.5   E 10.5

15   28   35   42   49   56   63   ?

   A 67   B 68   C 69   D 70   E 75

16   10   15   25   30   40   45   ?

   A 50   B 60   C 65   D 70   E 55

17   32   43   37   48   42   53   ?

   A 47   B 57   C 58   D 59   E 45

18   5   6   7   9   10   11   13   14   ?

   A 9   B 14   C 16   D 17   E 15

19   40   38   39   37   38   36   ?

   A 35   B 34   C 36   D 37   E 38

NUMBER ANALOGIES

How do they all go together?

Maya

Directions (read to child): Look at the first two sets of numbers. Try to come up with a rule that both of these sets of numbers follow. Take this rule and try to figure out which answer choice goes in the place of the question mark to complete the third set of numbers.

Parent note: A more detailed explanation and a Number Analogies example question is on p.20. If you have not already, look over p.20.

Number Analogies questions are in two forms: the form of #1 (3 sets aligned vertically with boxes around the numbers) or in the form of #8 (3 sets aligned horizontally with no boxes).

Example #1: In the first set of numbers, we see 8 and 7. In the second set, we see 6 and 5. How would you get from 8 to 7? How would you get from 6 to 5? In each, you take away 1 from the first number.

This could be the "rule" that both sets follow. Let's take this rule and apply it to the bottom set.

What is the answer when you have 10, and then take away 1? The answer is 9.

1

8	→	7
6	→	5
10	→	?

(A) 8　　　　(B) 11　　　(C) 3　　　(D) 9　　　(E) 4

2

4	→	8
3	→	6
5	→	?

A 10   B 9   C 8   D 12   E 11

3

35	→	38
45	→	48
25	→	?

A 26   B 27   C 28   D 29   E 30

4

2	→	8
5	→	20
6	→	?

A 25   B 24   C 22   D 21   E 12

5

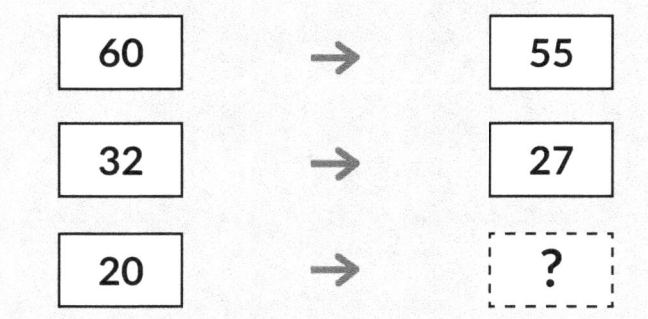

60	→	55
32	→	27
20	→	?

A 15   B 16   C 17   D 18   E 19

6

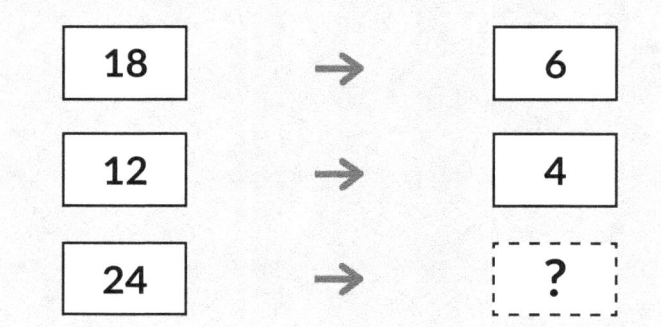

18	→	6
12	→	4
24	→	?

A 9   B 10   C 6   D 7   E 8

7

90	→	9
30	→	3
60	→	?

A 4   B 5   C 6   D 7   E 8

8   [25 → 32]   [20 → 27]   [15 → ?]

   A 12   B 17   C 21   D 22   E 7

9   [10 → 5]   [16 → 8]   [18 → ?]

   A 6   B 8   C 9   D 10   E 12

10   [70 → 60]   [60 → 50]   [10 → ?]

   A 0   B 10   C 20   D 30   E 50

11   [2 → 6]   [4 → 12]   [5 → ?]

   A 10   B 15   C 17   D 3   E 20

12   [12 → 0]   [20 → 8]   [30 → ?]

   A 14   B 18   C 20   D 10   E 12

13 [5 → 25] [6 → 36] [7 → ?]

Ⓐ 47 Ⓑ 7 Ⓒ 77 Ⓓ 42 Ⓔ 49

14 [10 → 20] [30 → 60] [11 → ?]

Ⓐ 80 Ⓑ 40 Ⓒ 20 Ⓓ 22 Ⓔ 111

15 [40 → 8] [30 → 6] [20 → ?]

Ⓐ 2 Ⓑ 4 Ⓒ 6 Ⓓ 5 Ⓔ 10

16 [8 → 14] [9 → 15] [10 → ?]

Ⓐ 17 Ⓑ 18 Ⓒ 16 Ⓓ 20 Ⓔ 21

17 [50 → 45] [45 → 40] [30 → ?]

Ⓐ 25 Ⓑ 30 Ⓒ 32 Ⓓ 40 Ⓔ 20

18 [3 → 18] [4 → 24] [5 → ?]

Ⓐ 25 Ⓑ 28 Ⓒ 3 Ⓓ 32 Ⓔ 30

COGAT® PRACTICE TEST 2

VERBAL ANALOGIES

The first set of words goes together in some way. Which answer choice would go in place of the question mark so that the second set goes together in the same way as the first set?

1   **write → paper : paint → ?**

(A) artist   (B) canvas   (C) brush   (D) color   (E) pencil

2   **rain → umbrella : sun → ?**

(A) cloud   (B) heat   (C) sky   (D) swimsuit   (E) hat

3   **morning → evening : spring → ?**

(A) April   (B) flowers   (C) summer   (D) wind   (E) vacation

4   **paint → brush : sew → ?**

(A) fabric   (B) shirt   (C) pants   (D) wool   (E) needle

5   **captain → ship : pilot → ?**

(A) truck   (B) airport   (C) jet   (D) sky   (E) wings

6   **dolphin → whale : cheetah → ?**

A lion   B kitten   C mammal   D pony   E predator

7   **ruby → gem : gold → ?**

A silver   B mine   C metal   D bronze   E ring

8   **horse → gallop : snake → ?**

A slither   B bite   C fang   D shed   E reptile

9   **harp → instrument : oak → ?**

A acorn   B tree   C squirrel   D forest   E branch

10   **year → month : hour → ?**

A year   B day   C minute   D number   E time

11   glove → hand : sock → ?

      (A) shoe   (B) foot   (C) toe   (D) leg   (E) pair

12   owl → hoot : lion → ?

      (A) pride   (B) chase   (C) mane   (D) roar   (E) savannah

13   classroom → teacher : kitchen → ?

      (A) dinner   (B) customer   (C) menu   (D) maid   (E) chef

14   coach → team : principal → ?

      (A) school   (B) student   (C) teacher   (D) office   (E) hall

15   narrow → wide : shallow → ?

      (A) full   (B) empty   (C) dry   (D) deep   (E) hollow

16   **painter → painting : poet → ?**

   A pen   B word   C encyclopedia   D paper   E poem

17   **Arctic → polar bear : desert → ?**

   A seal   B alligator   C camel   D koala bear   E grizzly bear

18   **mouse → mice : person → ?**

   A children   B group   C woman   D percent   E people

19   **inventor → invention : author → ?**

   A publisher   B word   C book   D page   E library

20   **angry → furious : tired → ?**

   A nap   B exhausted   C sleepy   D rest   E cranky

21   **sole → shoe : trunk → ?**

   A bark   B leaf   C tree   D soil   E branch

1 **ankle** **thigh** **hip**

   A elbow B shoulder C waist D stomach E knee

2 **rectangle** **square** **trapezoid**

   A triangle B circle C octagon D diamond E cylinder

3 **maple** **birch** **oak**

   A flower B forest C leaf D pine E bush

4 **lungs** **heart** **liver**

   A stomach B muscle C blood D waist E body

5 **crawl** **walk** **run**

   A skip B movement C stand D lay E sleep

6   **carrot**   **onion**   **potato**

ᴬ lettuce   ᴮ radish   ᶜ cherry   ᴰ pasta   ᴱ corn

7   **wool**   **lace**   **silk**

ᴬ jacket   ᴮ dress   ᶜ cotton   ᴰ shirt   ᴱ fabric

8   **Saturn**   **Mars**   **Neptune**

ᴬ Moon   ᴮ Sun   ᶜ Jupiter   ᴰ Milky Way   ᴱ Haley's Comet

9   **dentist**   **surgeon**   **nurse**

ᴬ firefighter   ᴮ pilot   ᶜ police officer   ᴰ cashier   ᴱ doctor

10   **whisper**   **shout**   **mumble**

ᴬ volume   ᴮ yell   ᶜ speech   ᴰ conversation   ᴱ words

11 **skyscraper**   **apartment**   **cabin**

(A) ceiling   (B) hut   (C) attic   (D) plan   (E) living room

12 **feathers**   **hair**   **fur**

(A) scales   (B) jacket   (C) crab   (D) beaches   (E) leaves

13 **cherry**   **pear**   **peach**

(A) watermelon   (B) strawberry   (C) grape   (D) apple   (E) fruit

14 **eagle**   **hawk**   **falcon**

(A) sparrow   (B) bird   (C) vulture   (D) robin   (E) hummingbird

15 **soup**   **stew**   **broth**

(A) water   (B) ice cream   (C) bowl   (D) chili   (E) sauce

16   **brake**   **engine**   **wheel**

  A car   B truck   C radio   D highway   E tire

17   **cactus**   **grass**   **apricot**

  A soil   B lily   C branch   D garden   E greenhouse

18   **circle**   **loop**   **ring**

  A angle   B spiral   C triangle   D rectangle   E curve

19   **shoulder**   **knee**   **elbow**

  A lips   B nose   C wrist   D stomach   E chest

20   **whisper**   **sigh**   **hum**

  A shout   B yell   C squeal   D roar   E mumble

SENTENCE COMPLETION
A word in the sentence is missing. Which choice best completes the sentence?

1 To make the pancake batter, we had to _____ milk, eggs, and flour in a large bowl.

   A separate   B eat   C blend   D cook   E consume

2 The final round between the top two _____ will decide which one wins the championship.

   A fans   B games   C umpires   D referees   E opponents

3 As we continued deeper into the forest that morning, the tall trees blocked the sky and the sunlight _____.

   A disappeared   B brightened   C glowed   D shone   E returned

4 The nurse will _____ a cream to help the cut heal faster.

   A measure   B apply   C discard   D discover   E invent

5 Putting a lid on the pot will help _____ the steam.

   A release   B escape   C cook   D trap   E heat

82

6   Because of the _____ temperatures, ice might _____ on the roads.

A cold,   B freezing,   C chilly,   D warm,   E high,
   melt   form   slip   develop   appear

7   After _____ the balloons, we had to _____ them so they wouldn't float away.

A flying,   B tying,   C inflating,   D filling up,   E bursting,
   color   pierce   tie   cut   flatten

8   A good_____ for improving soccer skills is to practice passing and dribbling every day.

A reason   B score   C coach   D method   E player

9   If more students join the art club, we'll need to bring _____ paint brushes.

A extra   B less   C reduced   D smaller   E colorful

10   We need to _____ the rules of the game so that players who speak other languages can understand them also.

A yell   B mix   C send   D copy   E translate

11 The thunderstorm caused a _____ increase in rainfall.

    Ⓐ gentle   Ⓑ tiny   Ⓒ sudden   Ⓓ peaceful   Ⓔ small

12 Your lungs and heart are _____ for your body's survival.

    Ⓐ useless   Ⓑ extra   Ⓒ helpful   Ⓓ necessary   Ⓔ scientific

13 It is _____ to have water when _____ on a hot day outside.

    Ⓐ optional, exercising   Ⓑ free, inside   Ⓒ essential, hiking   Ⓓ avoidable, running   Ⓔ confusing, jogging

14 The judges will _____ each figure skater's performance during the show.

    Ⓐ assess   Ⓑ cheer   Ⓒ coach   Ⓓ copy   Ⓔ finish

15 Since I wasn't involved in the game, I sat in the stands as a _____.

    Ⓐ coach   Ⓑ player   Ⓒ referee   Ⓓ judge   Ⓔ spectator

16   Because the books were so popular, as soon as new copies _____, customers _____ them all.

A printed,
   replaced

B sold,
   returned

C arrived,
   purchased

D appeared,
   avoided

E came,
   rejected

17   We _____ bad traffic following the concert, so we left early.

A avoided

B wanted

C created

D expected

E ignored

18   Instead of long and detailed, the book's summary is _____.

A clear

B messy

C confusing

D brief

E creative

19   If the eye drops _____ your eyes, you should not _____ them.

A irritate,
   use

B bother,
   avoid

C soothe,
   use

D improve,
   spread

E help,
   buy

20   The temperature at the beach is _____, so we packed both swimsuits and sweaters.

A steady

B rainy

C regular

D warm

E unpredictable

FIGURE ANALOGIES

Directions: The pictures in the top boxes go together in some way. One of the bottom boxes is empty. Which answer choice goes with the picture in the bottom box in the same way the top pictures do?

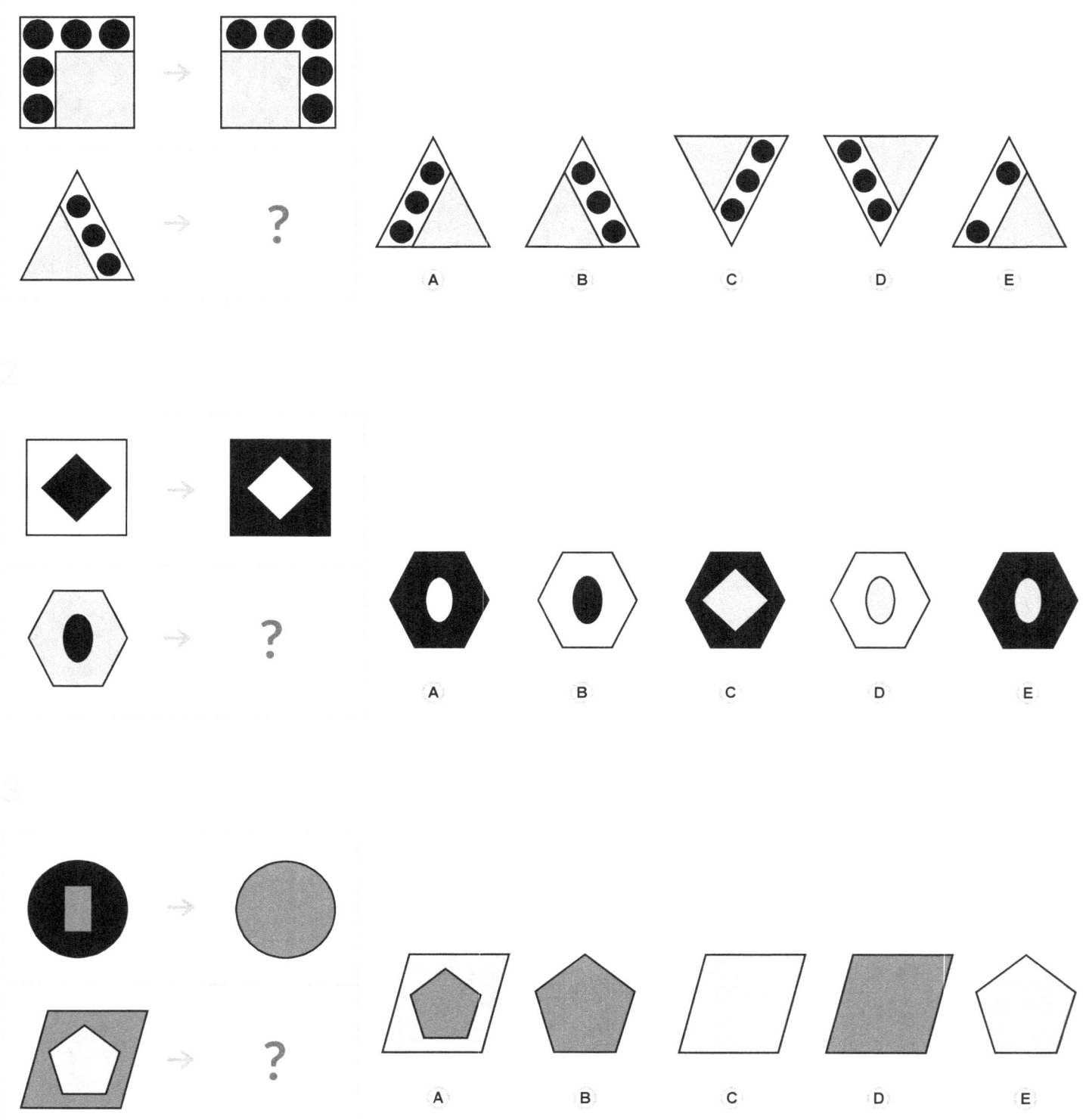

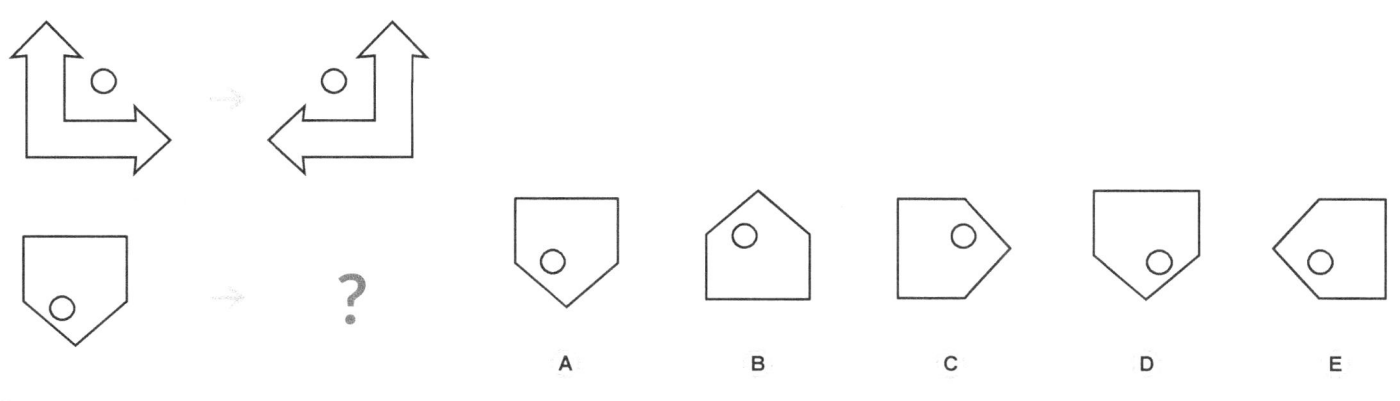

A B C D E

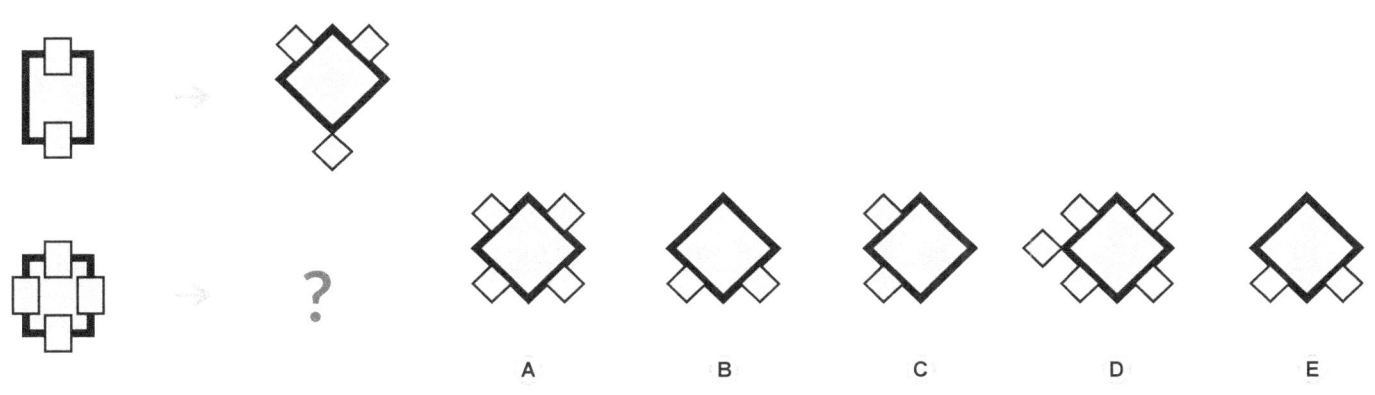

A B C D E

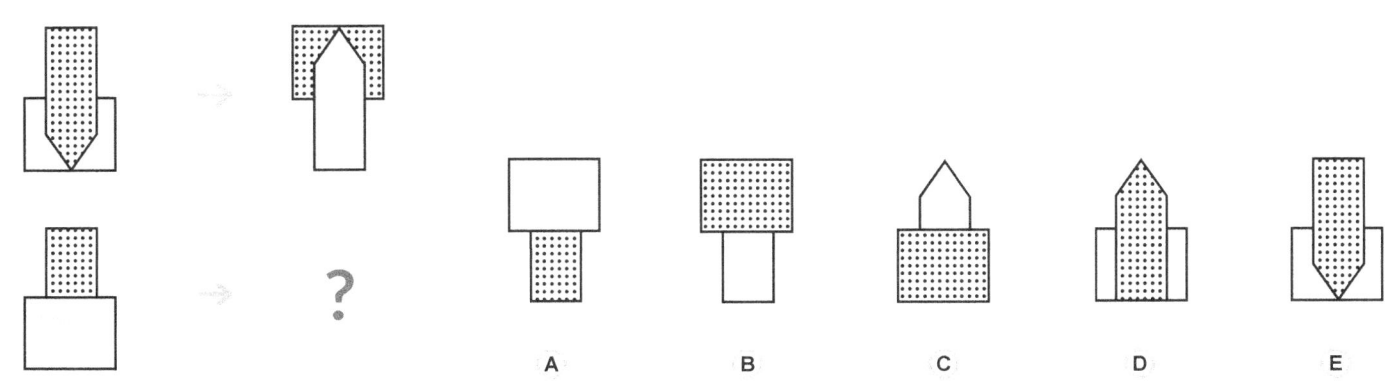

A B C D E

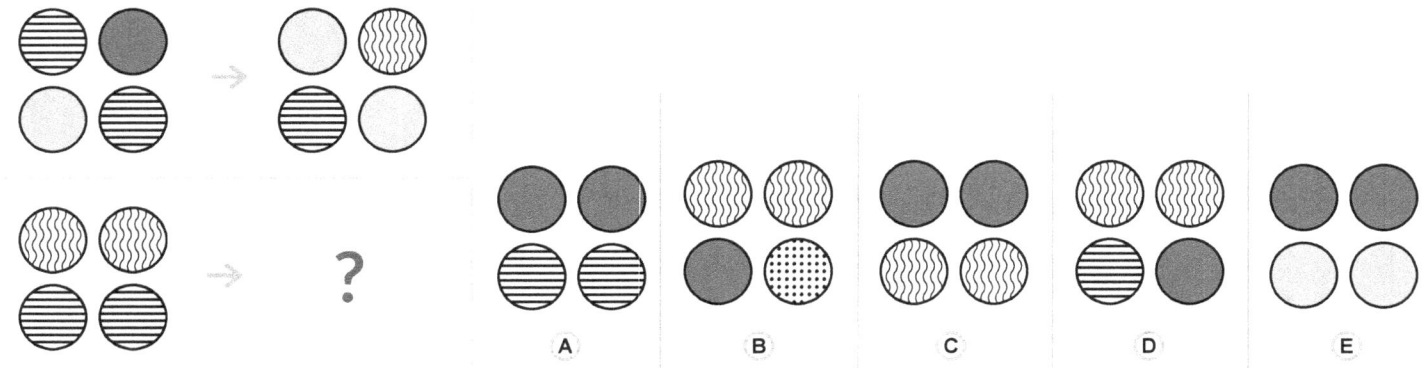

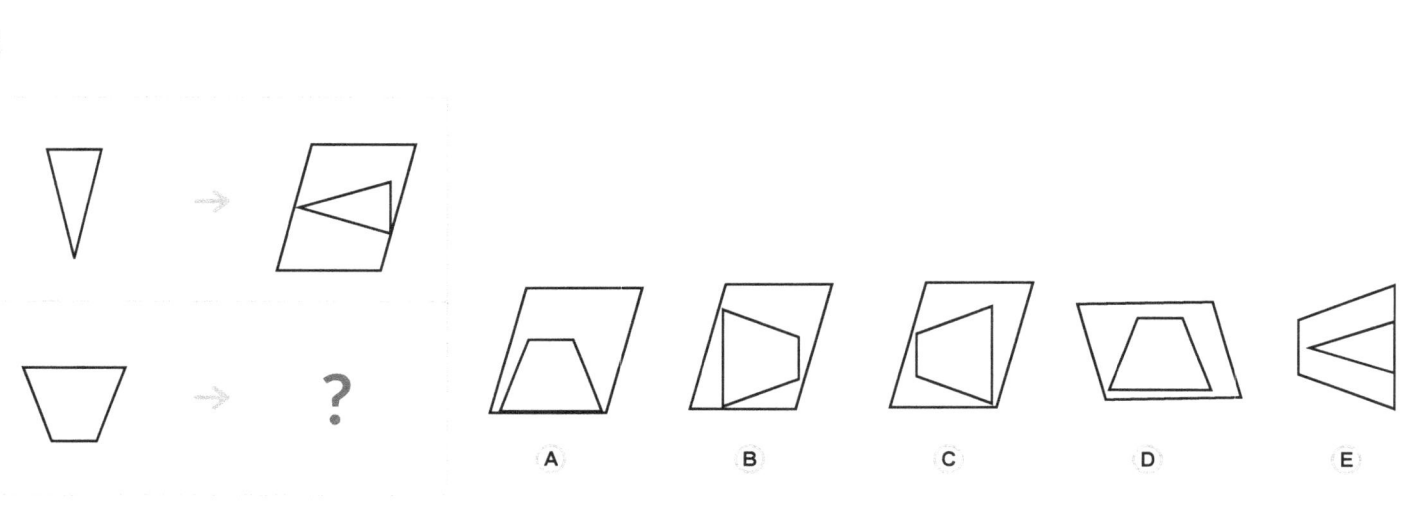

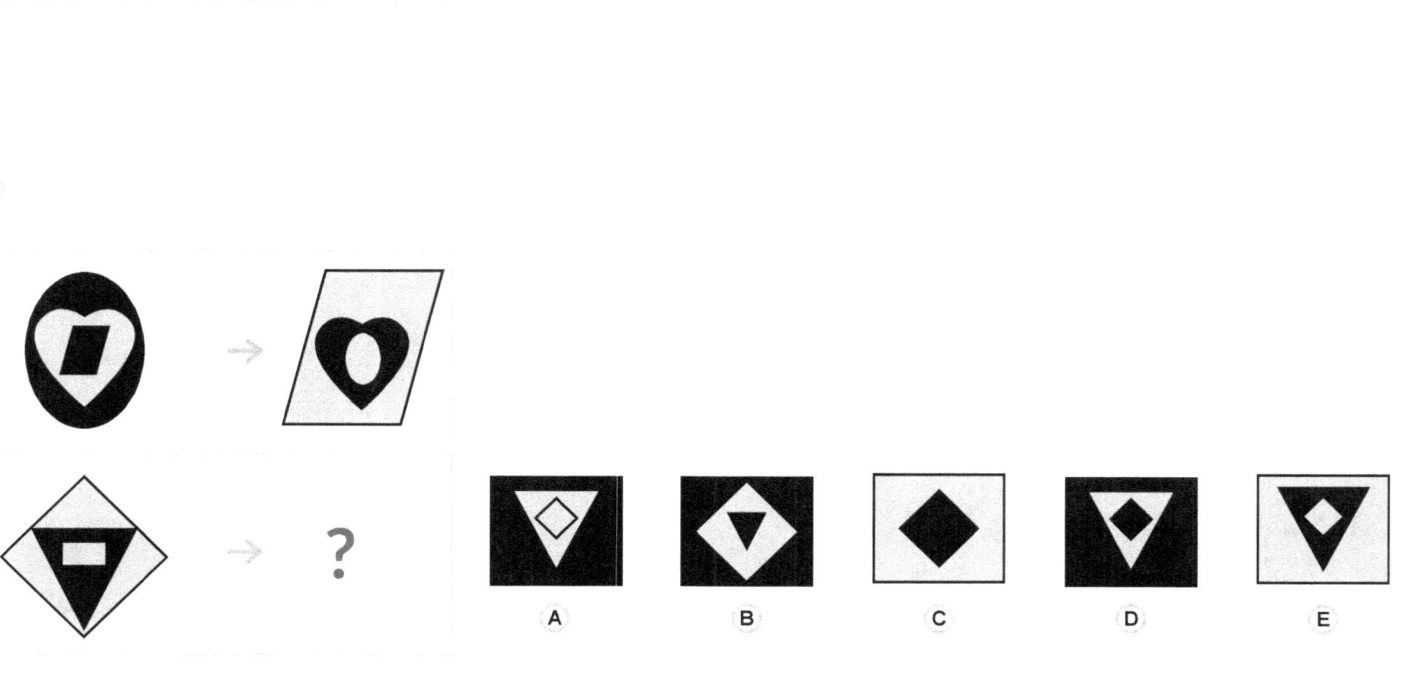

88

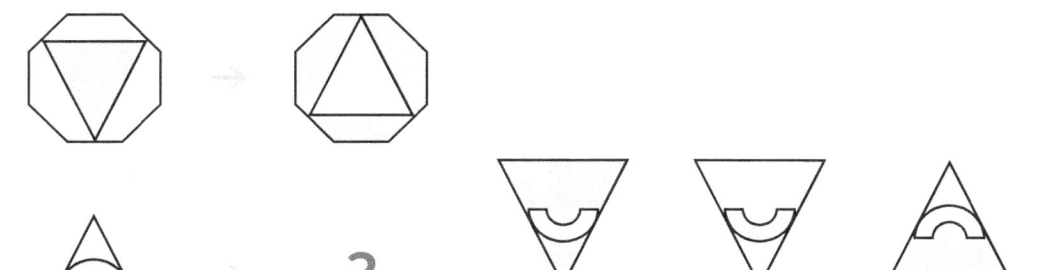

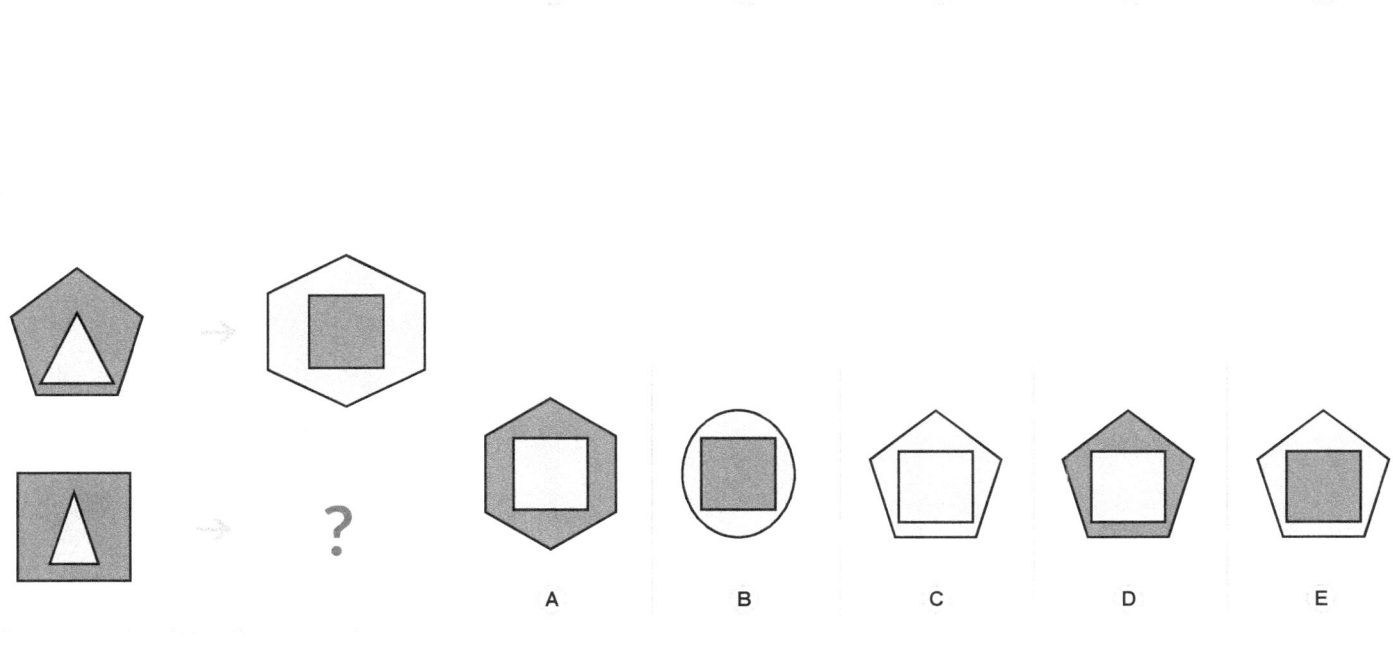

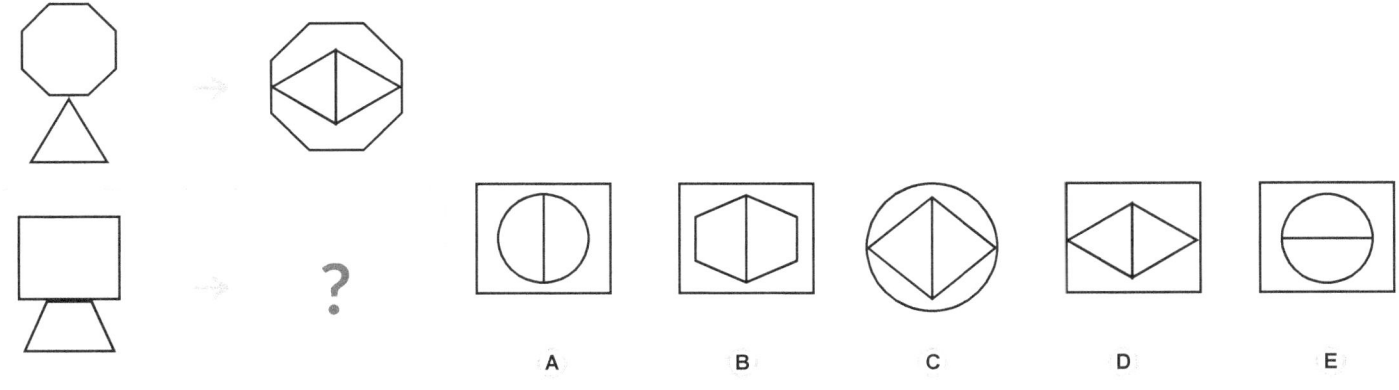

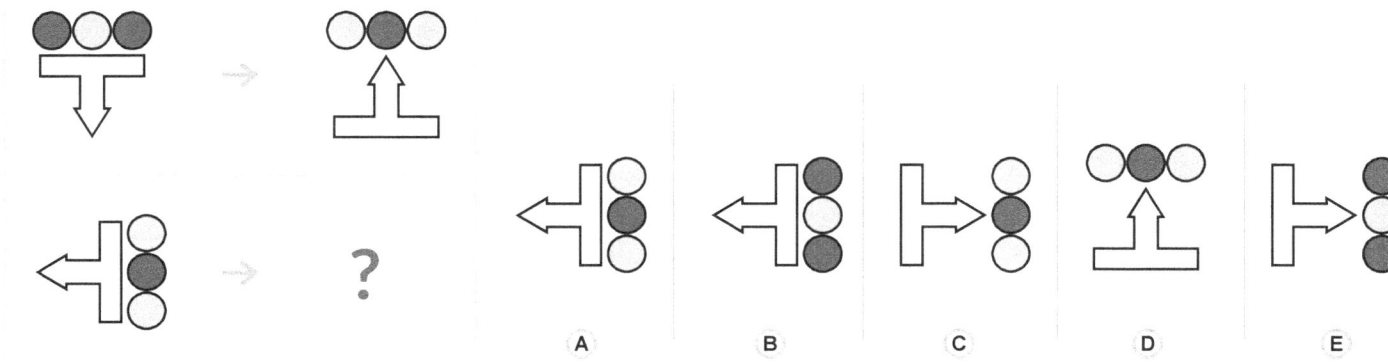

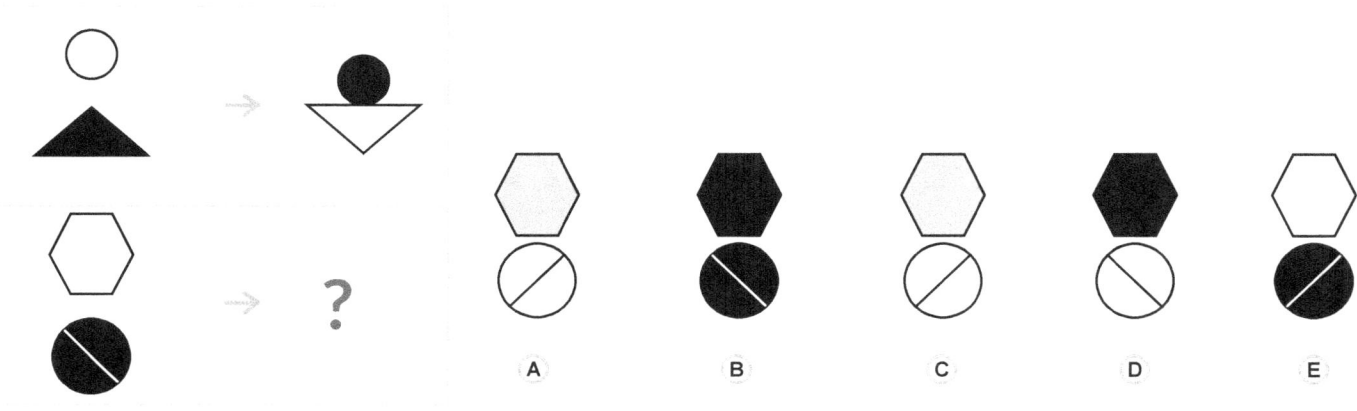

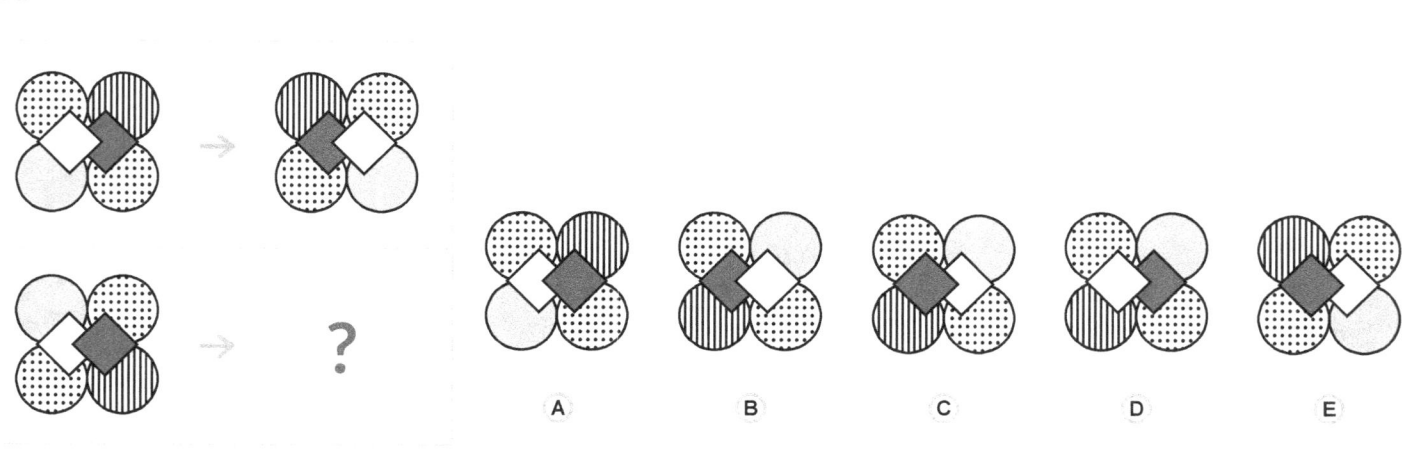

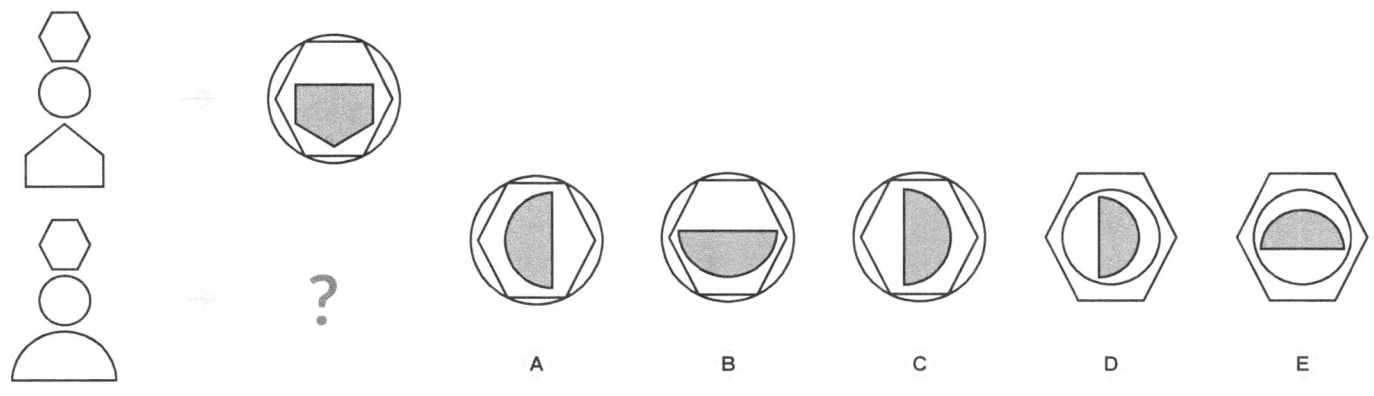

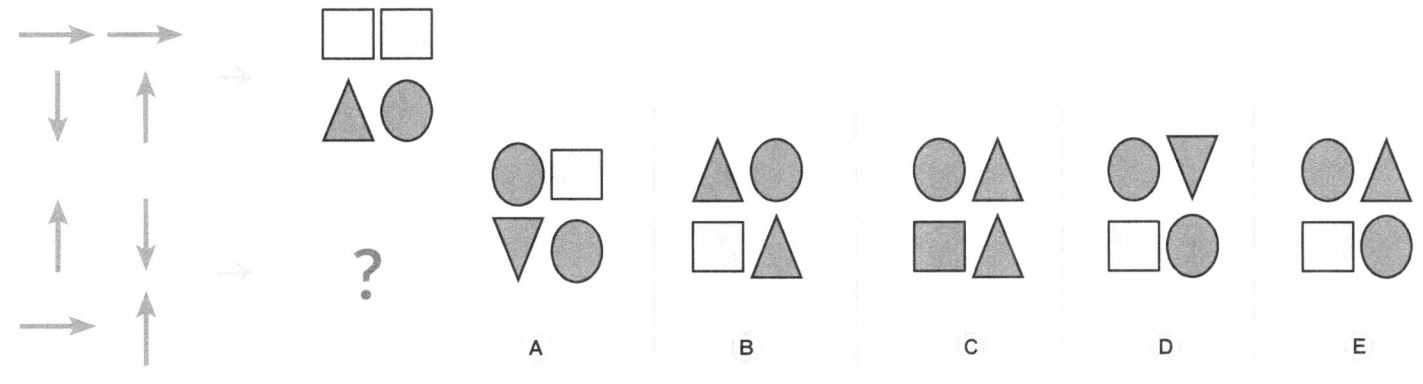

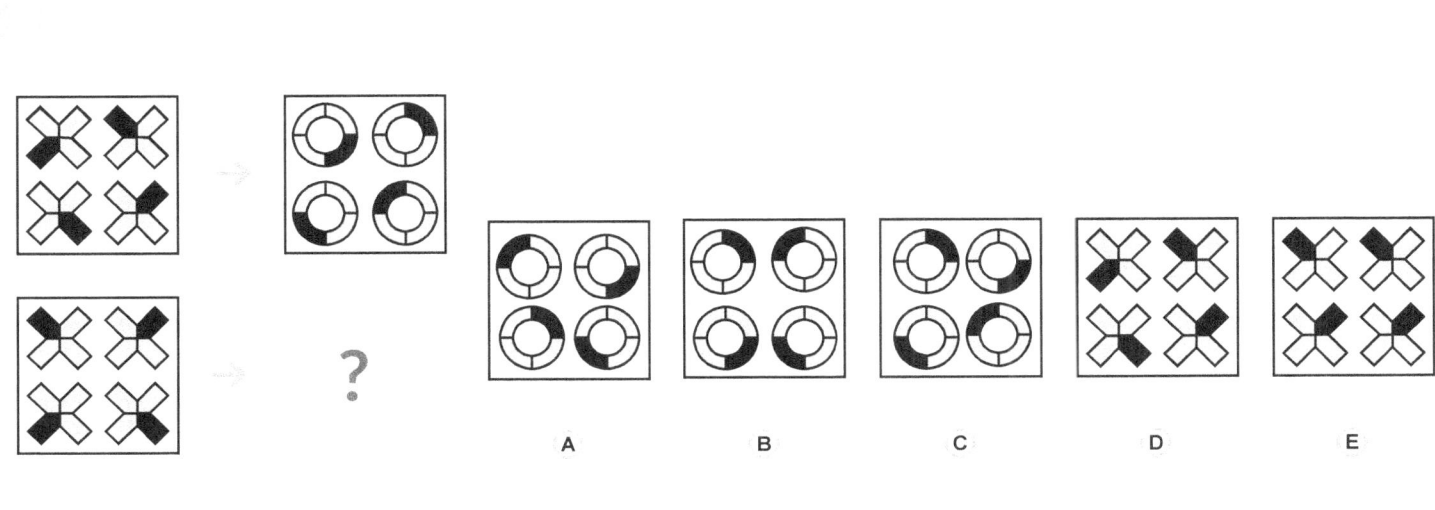

FIGURE CLASSIFICATION

Directions: The top row shows three pictures that are alike in some way. Look at the bottom row. Which bottom picture goes best with the top pictures?

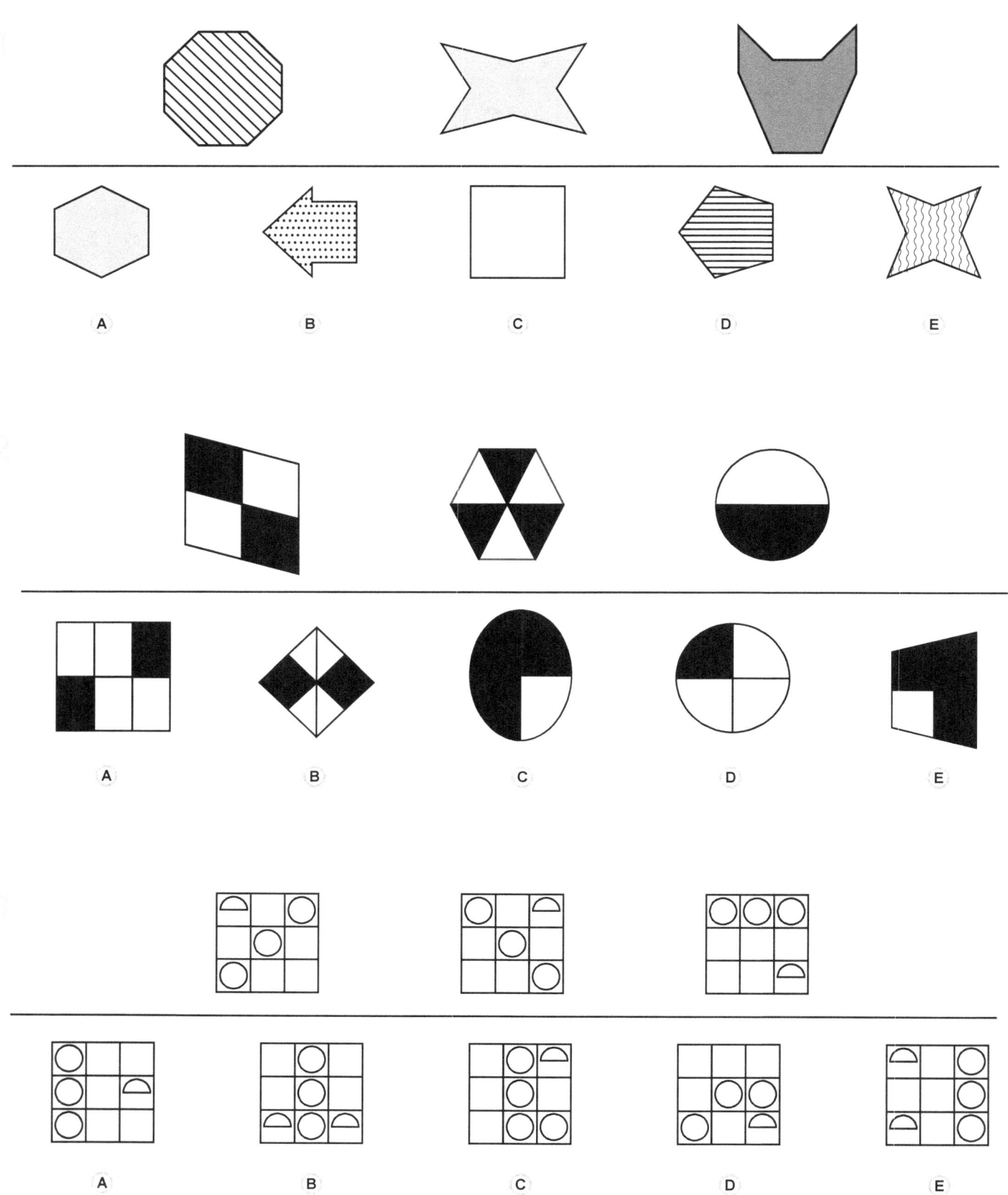

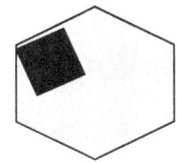  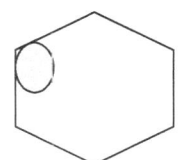

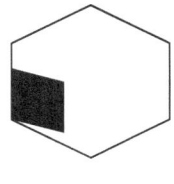 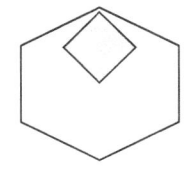 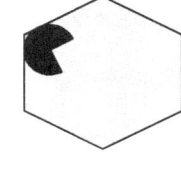 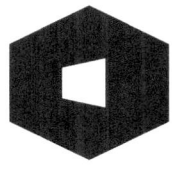 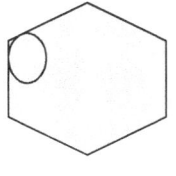

A B C D E

 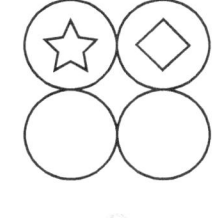 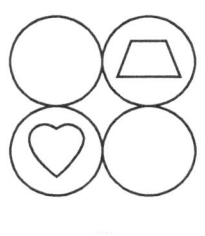  

A B C D E

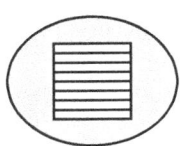 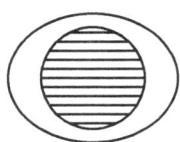 

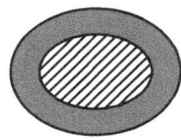 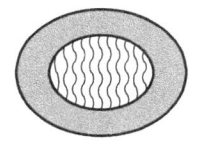  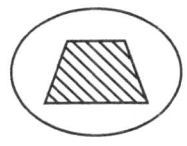 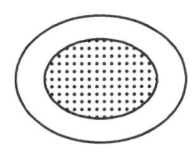

A B C D E

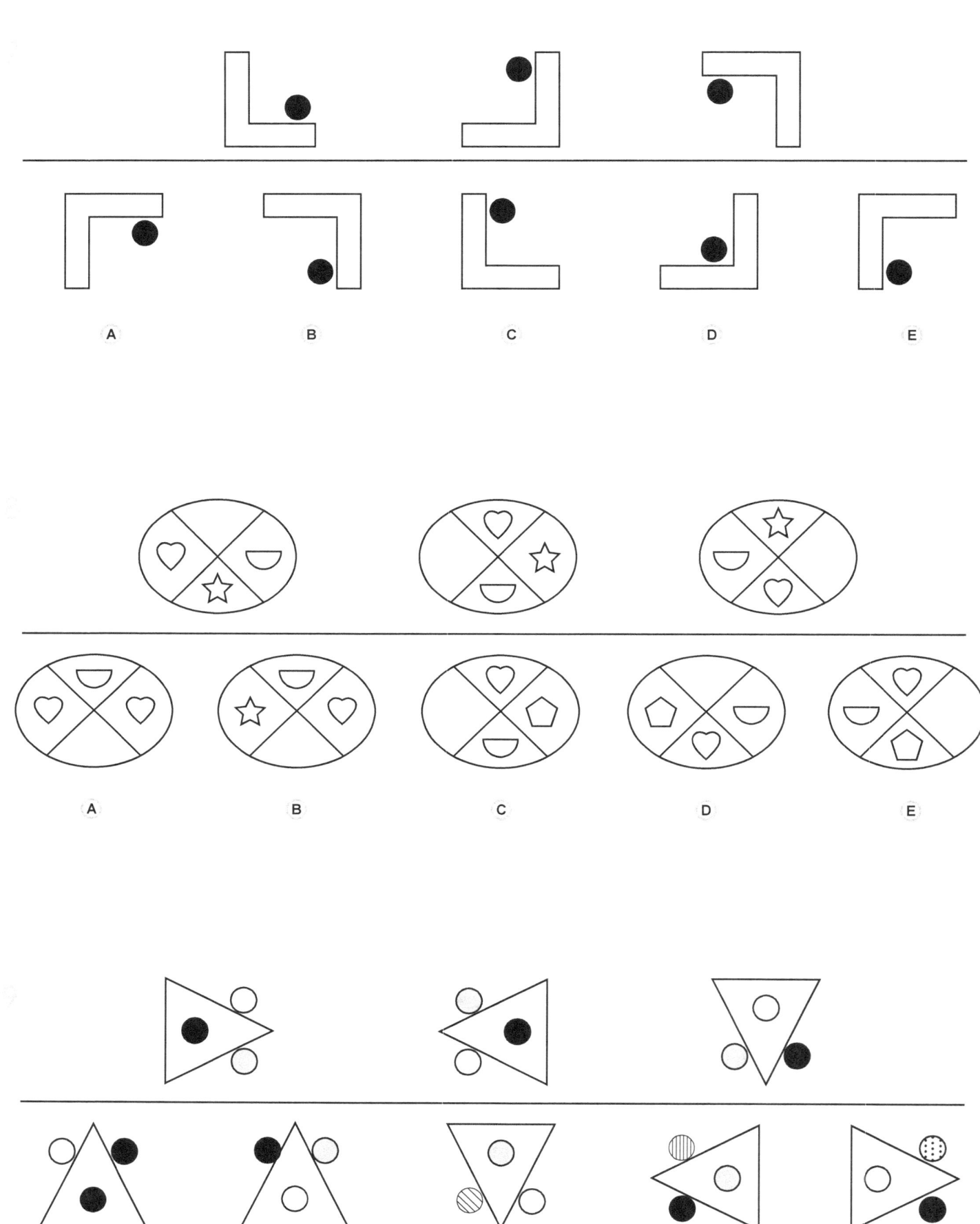

  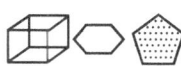

 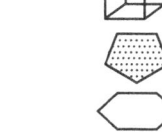 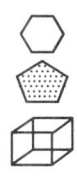 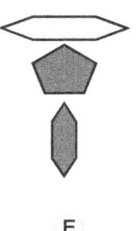

A   B   C   D   E

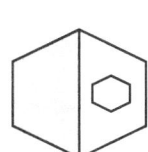 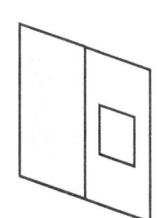

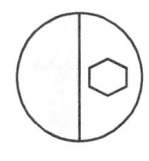 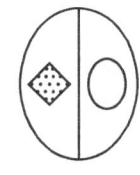 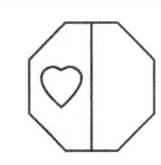 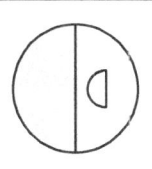 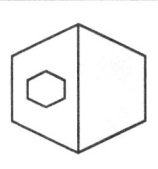

A   B   C   D   E

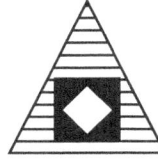 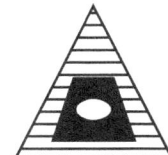 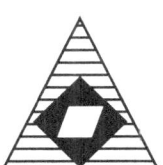

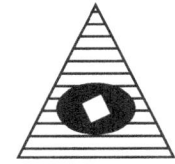 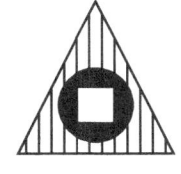 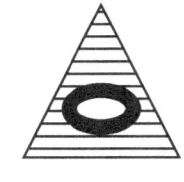 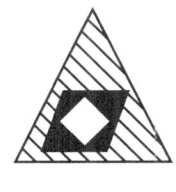 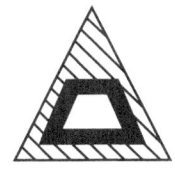

A   B   C   D   E

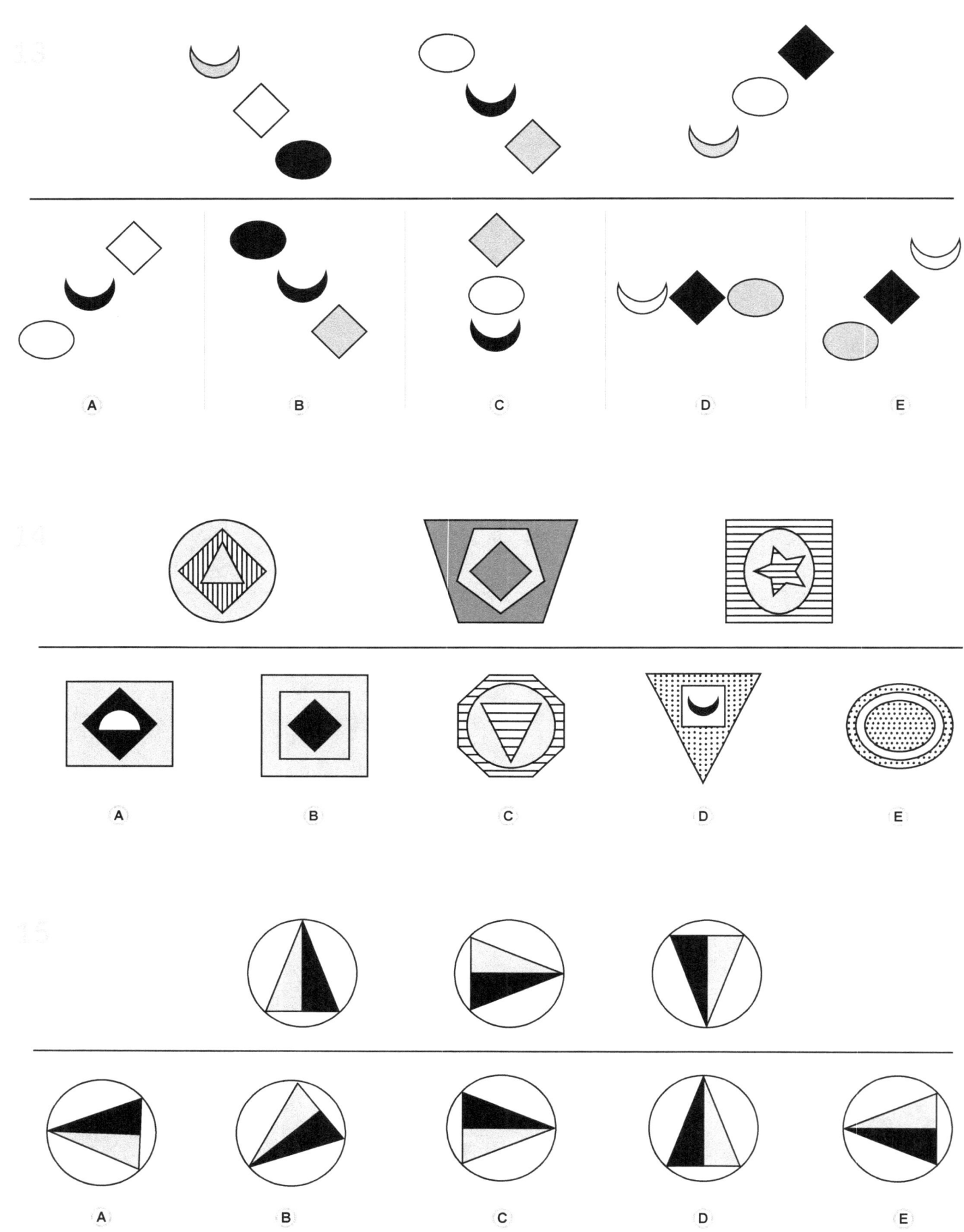

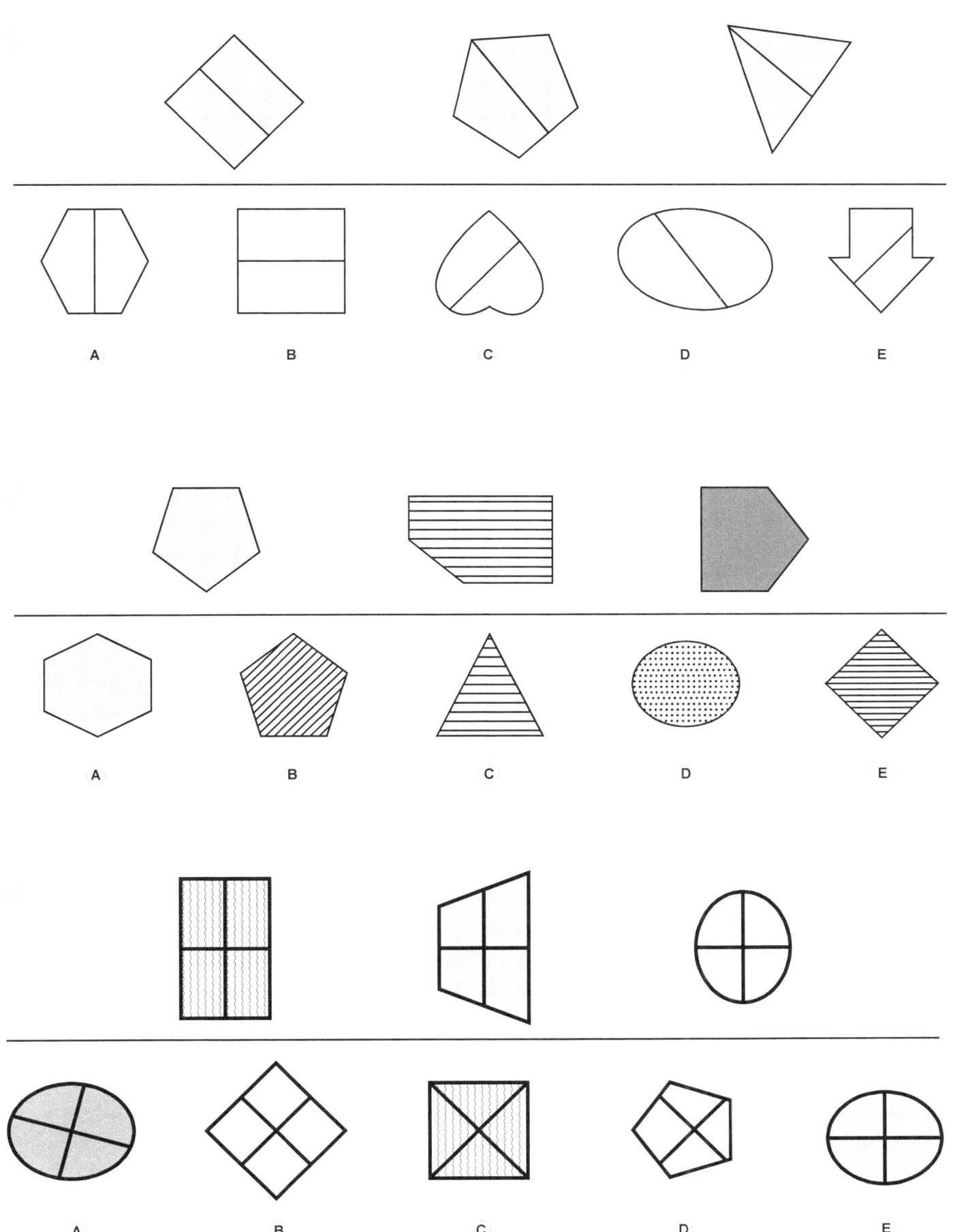

A   B   C   D   E

A   B   C   D   E

A   B   C   D   E

97

PAPER FOLDING

The top row of pictures shows a sheet of paper. The paper was folded, then something was cut out. Which picture in the bottom row shows how the paper would look after its unfolded?

1.

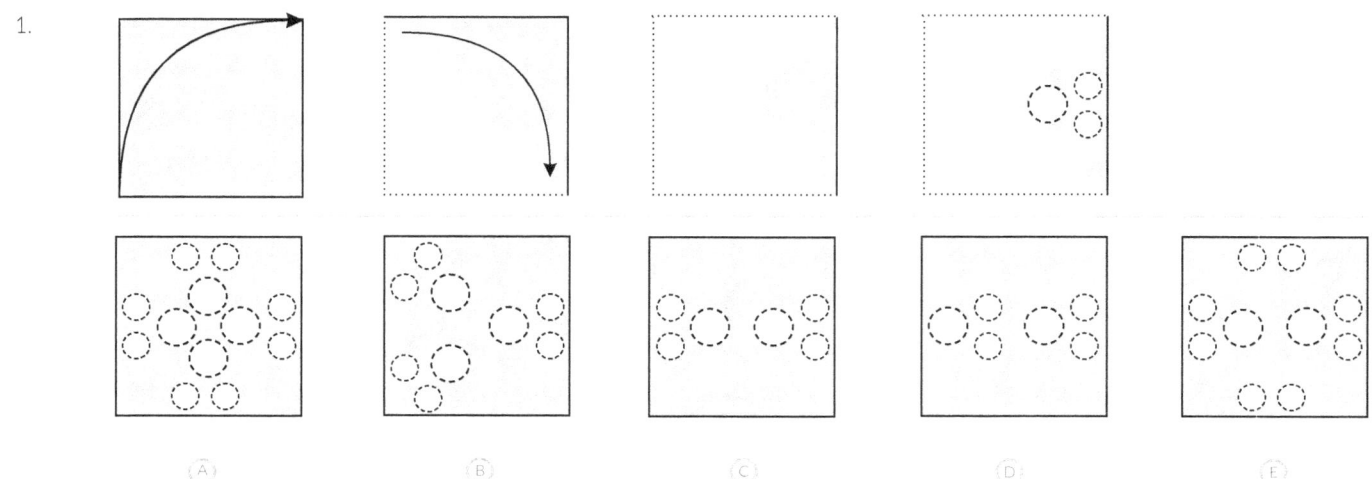

2.

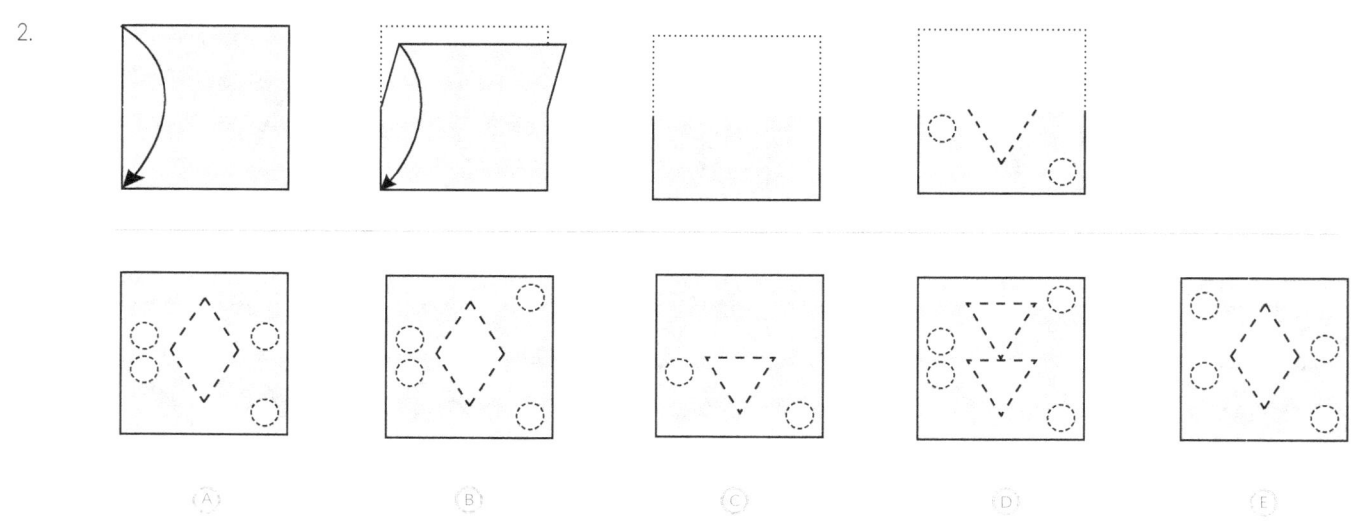

3.

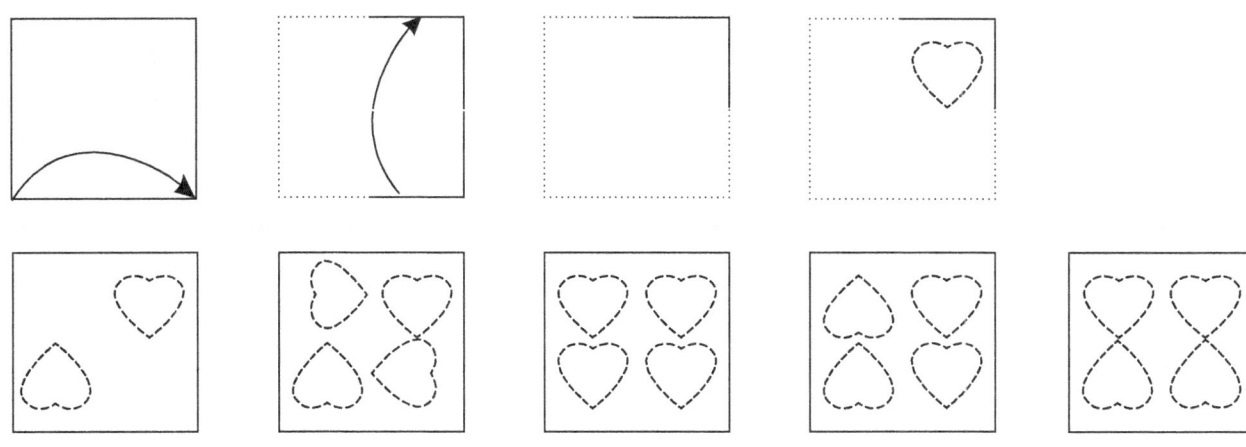

4.

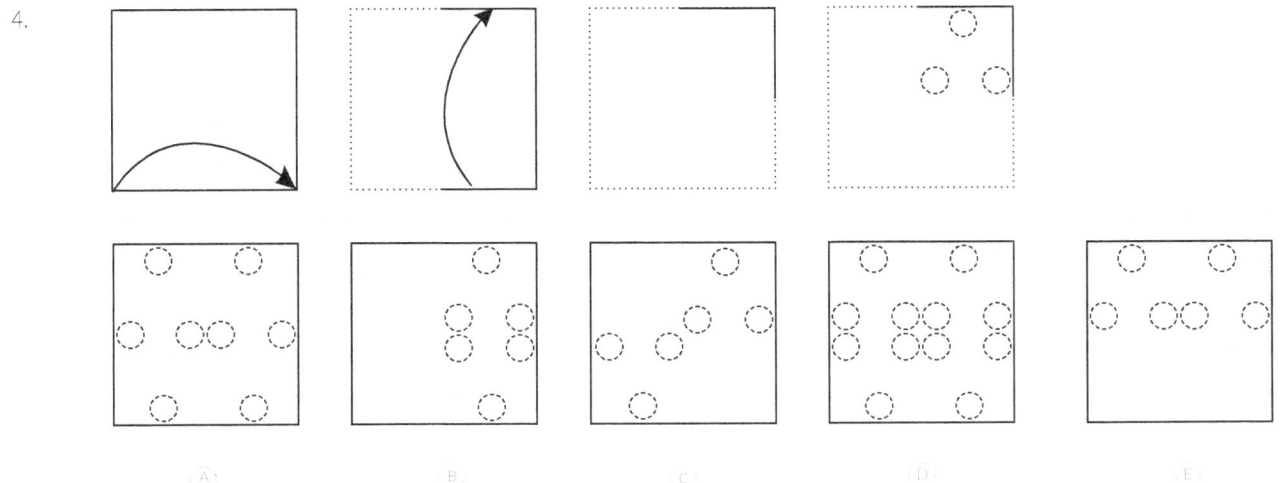

5.

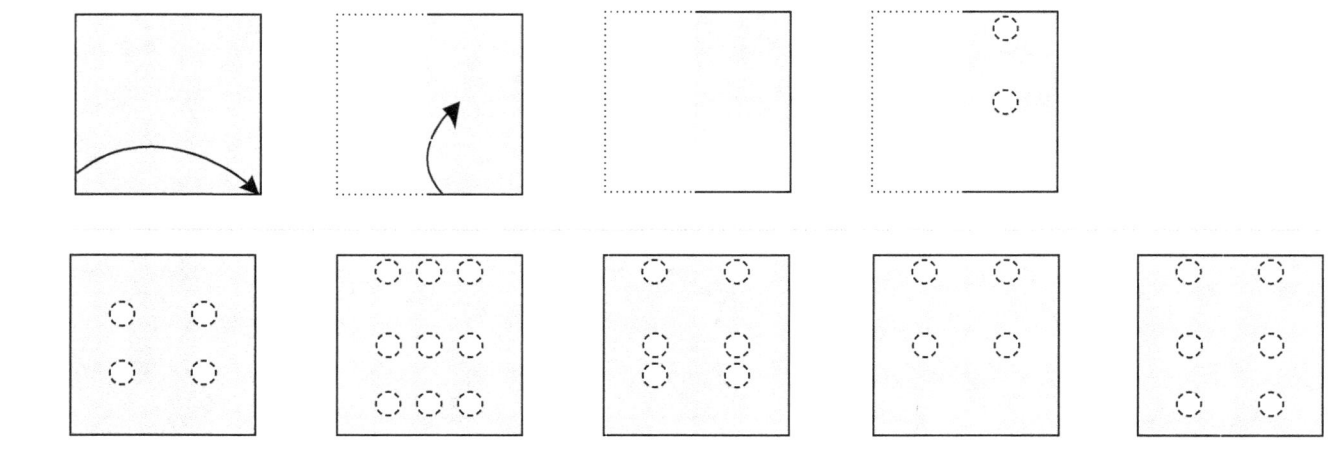

6.

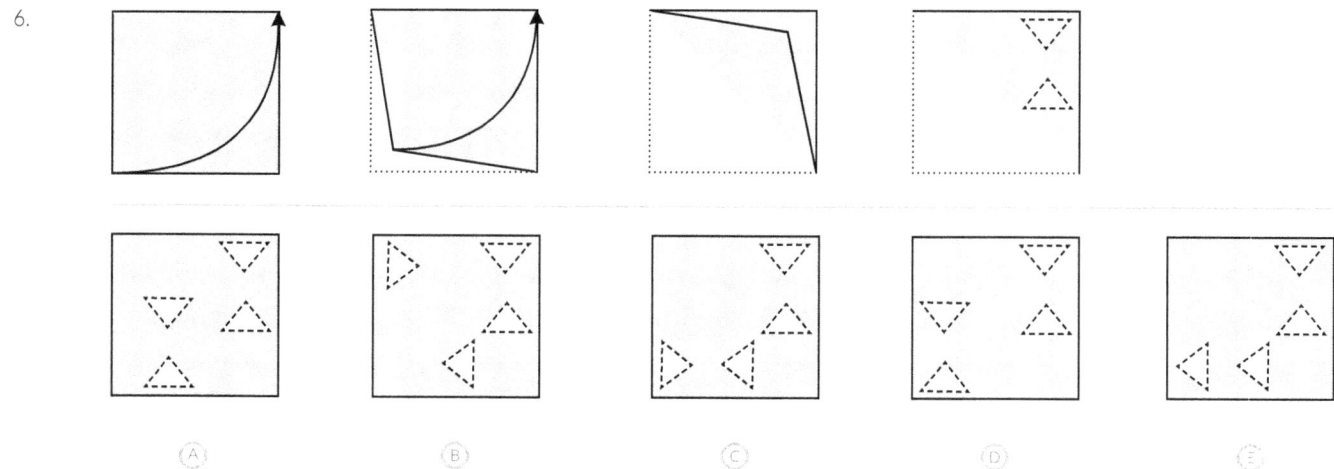

7.

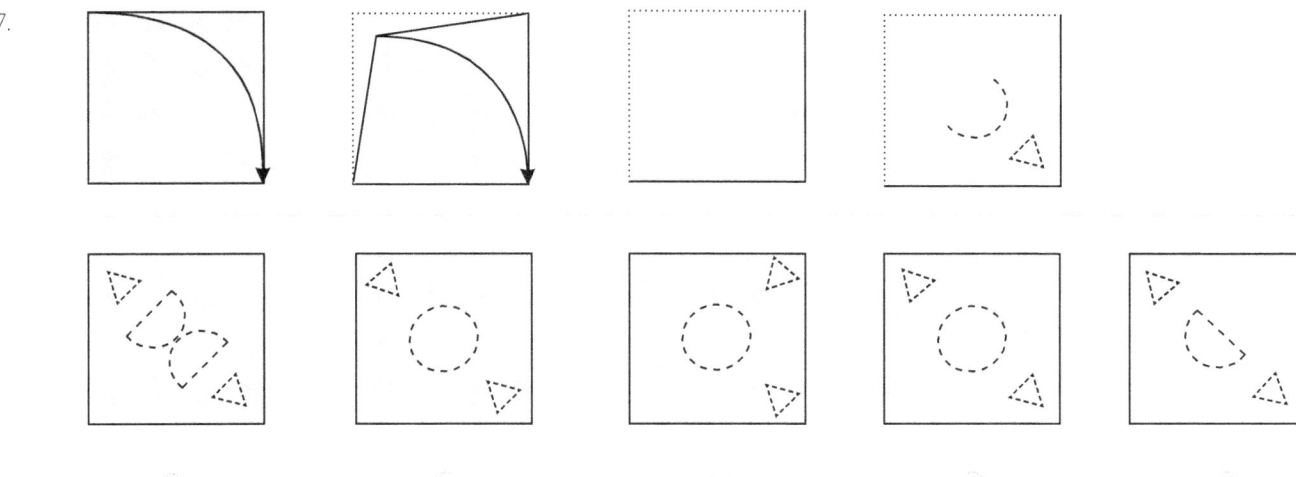

8.

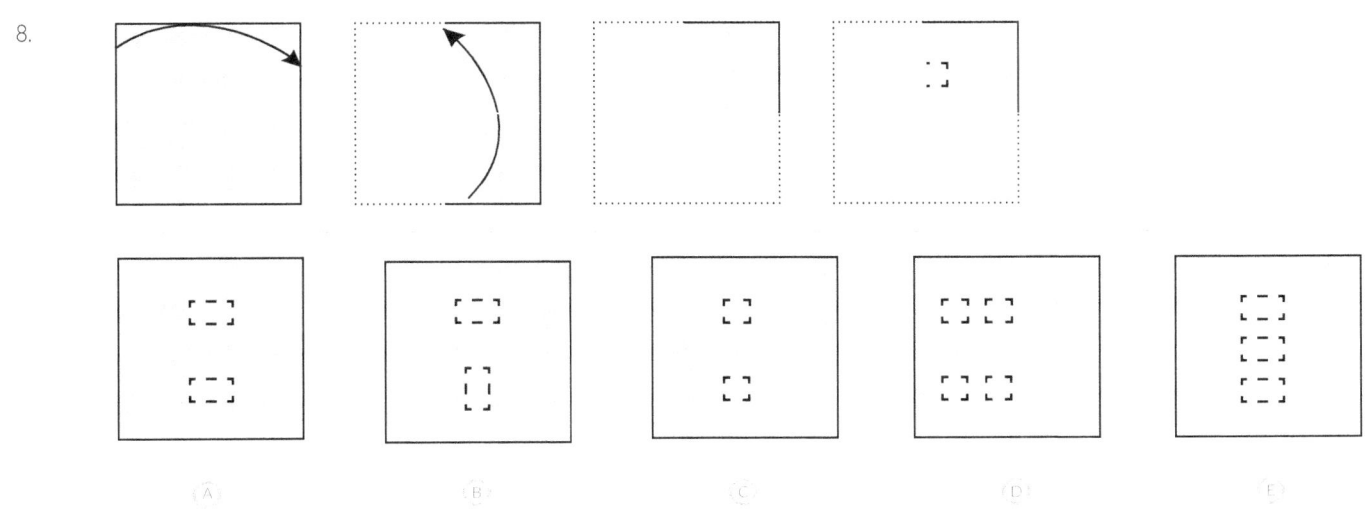

9.

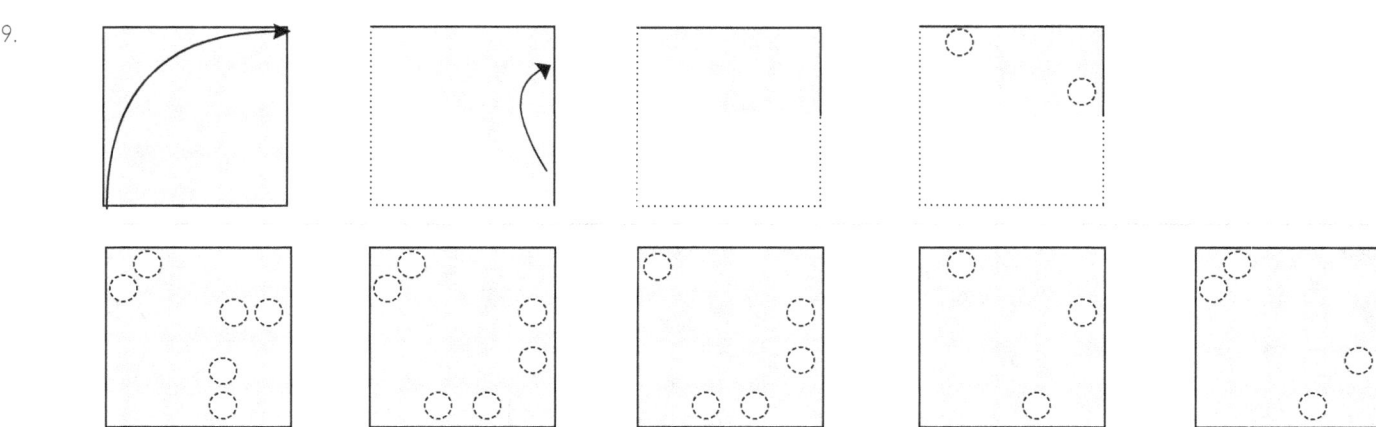

(A) (B) (C) (D) (E)

10.

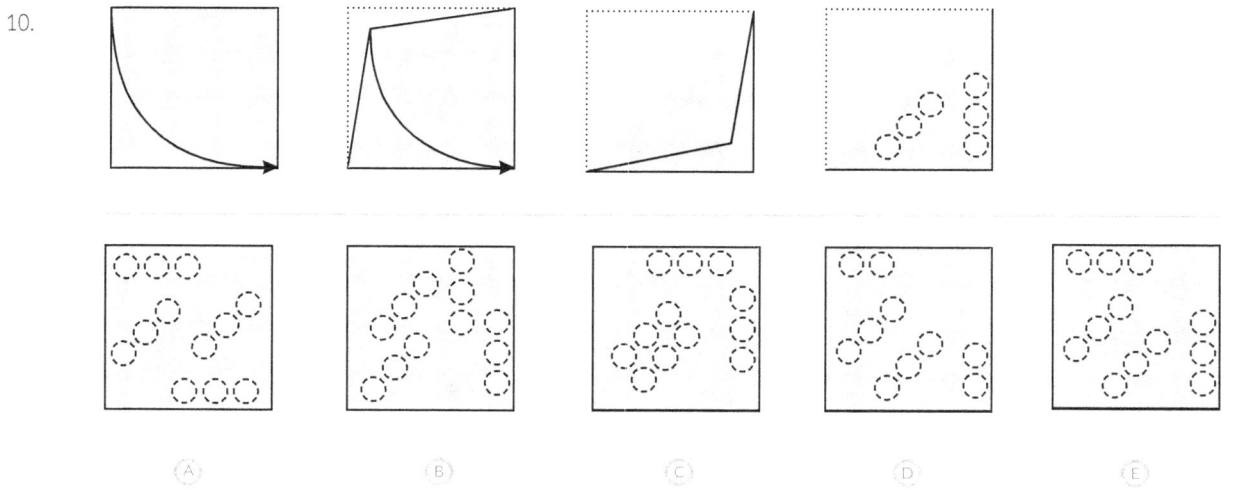

(A) (B) (C) (D) (E)

11.

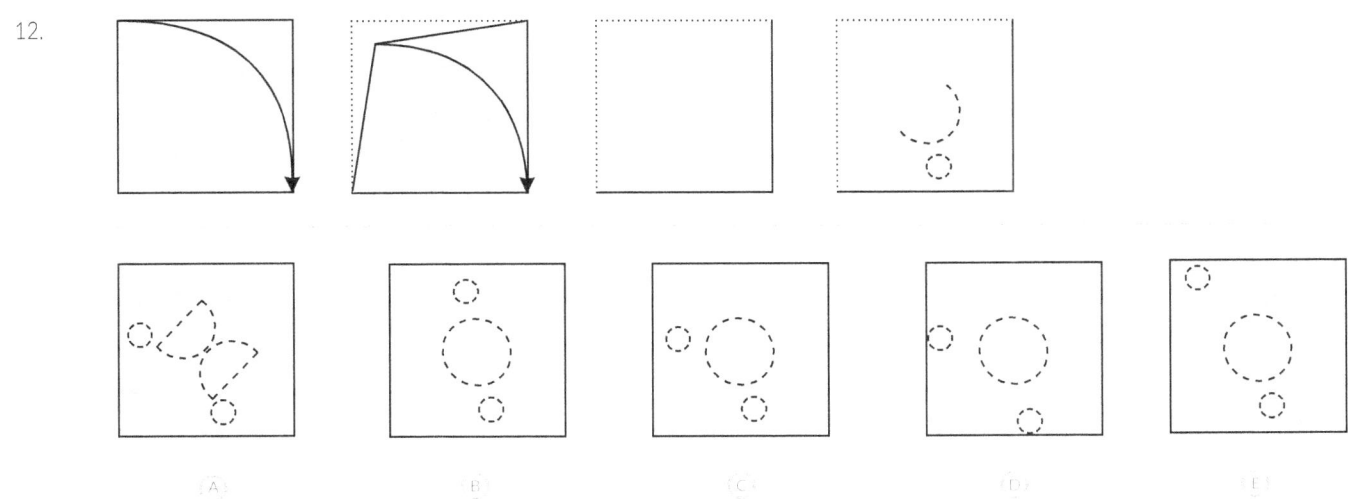

13.

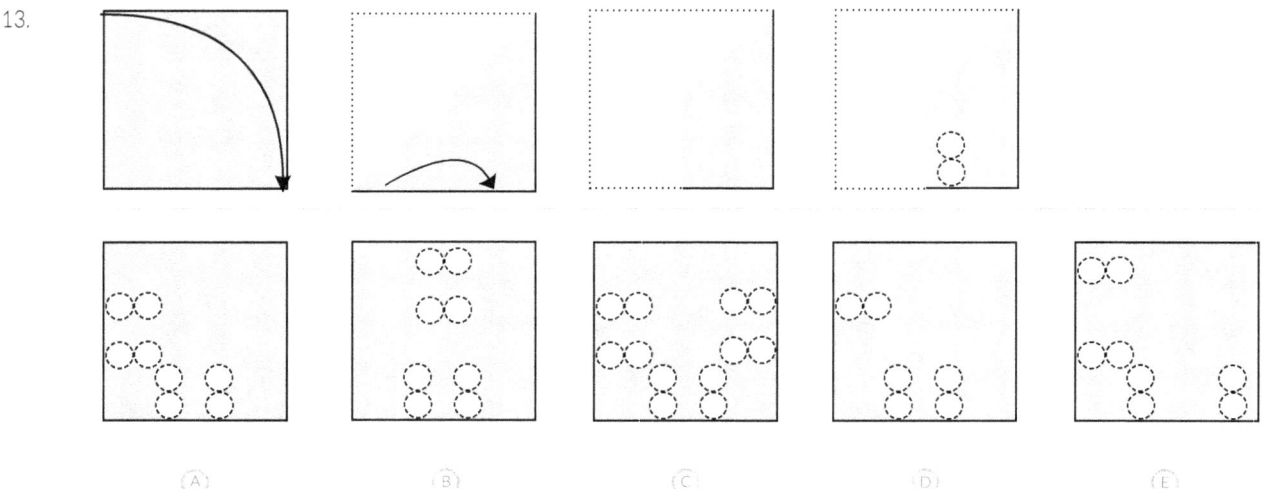

14.

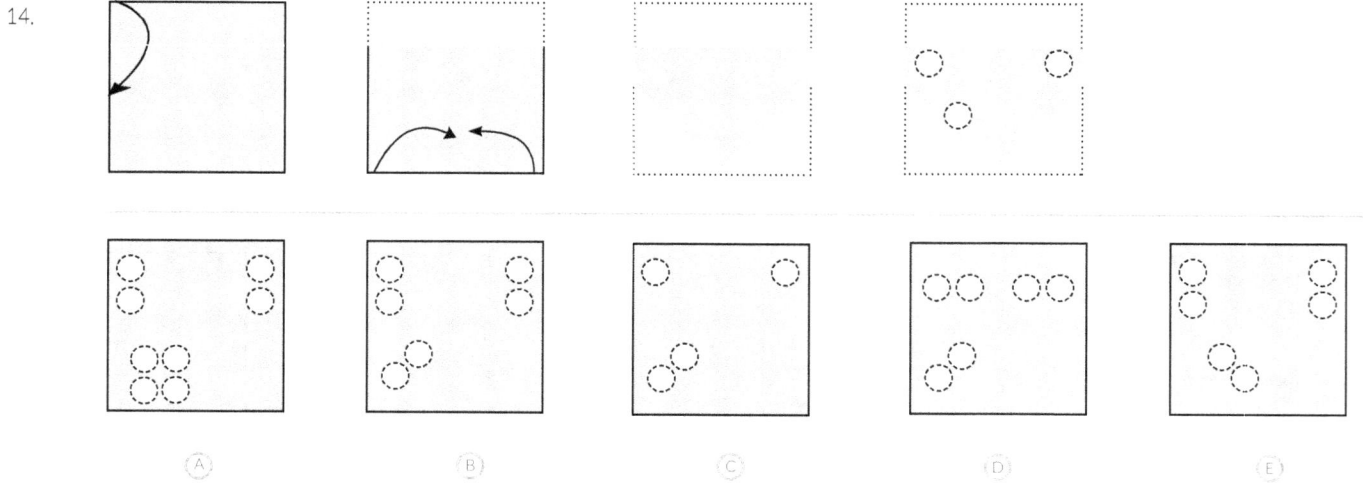

NUMBER PUZZLES

Directions: Which number would go in place of the question mark so that both of sides of the equal sign (point to the equal sign) have the same amount?

1

$9 \quad = \quad 63 \quad \div \quad \boxed{?}$

A 6   B 7   C 8   D 9   E 54

2

$45 \quad - \quad 27 \quad = \quad 72 \quad \div \quad \boxed{?}$

A 1   B 0   C 5   D 6   E 4

3

$\boxed{?} \quad + \quad 11 \quad = \quad 92 \quad - \quad 18$

A 74   B 62   C 63   D 64   E 81

4

$7 \quad \times \quad 6 \quad = \quad 30 \quad + \quad \boxed{?}$

A 10   B 12   C 14   D 15   E 18

5

$9 \quad \times \quad 5 \quad = \quad 63 \quad - \quad \boxed{?}$

A 49   B 16   C 17   D 18   E 45

6

$$99 \div 11 = \boxed{?} \div 3$$

A 27   B 9   C 30   D 33   E 36

7

$$15 \times 4 = \boxed{?} \times 5$$

A 60   B 10   C 11   D 12   E 15

8

$$48 \div 6 = \boxed{?} \div 2$$

A 108   B 16   C 8   D 20   E 24

9

$$\boxed{?} + 5 = \blacklozenge$$
$$10 + \blacklozenge = 22$$

A 5   B 6   C 7   D 8   E 9

10

$$\boxed{?} = \blacklozenge + 4$$
$$3 \times \blacklozenge = 21$$

A 9   B 10   C 11   D 12   E 13

11

$$\boxed{?} \times 2 = \blacklozenge$$
$$\blacklozenge \div 4 = 5$$

A 10   B 9   C 1   D 11   E 20

12

$$\boxed{?} = \blacklozenge \div 2$$
$$\blacklozenge - 20 = 14$$

A 6   B 36   C 34   D 8   E 17

13

$$\blacklozenge \div \boxed{?} = 4$$
$$2 + \blacklozenge = 30$$

A 5   B 6   C 11   D 8   E 7

14

$$\boxed{?} - \blacklozenge = 7$$
$$\blacklozenge \times 2 = 36$$

A 10   B 25   C 12   D 13   E 8

15

$$\blacklozenge + \boxed{?} = 20$$
$$\blacklozenge \div 5 = 3$$

A 4   B 15   C 6   D 5   E 8

16

$$\boxed{?} = \blacklozenge \div 4$$
$$\blacklozenge - 8 = 24$$

(A) 32   (B) 7   (C) 8   (D) 9   (E) 4

17

$$\boxed{?} = \blacklozenge + 7$$
$$10 = \blacklozenge + \bullet$$
$$\bullet = 4$$

(A) 11   (B) 13   (C) 6   (D) 5   (E) 4

18

$$\boxed{?} = \blacklozenge + 6$$
$$15 = \blacklozenge - \bullet$$
$$\bullet = 2$$

(A) 23   (B) 13   (C) 17   (D) 7   (E) 6

Directions: Which answer choice would complete the pattern?

1. 75 74 72 69 65 60 54 47 ?

A) 41 B) 40 C) 42 D) 38 E) 39

2. 5 10 20 5 10 20 ?

A) 0 B) 25 C) 5 D) 10 E) 15

3. 1 2 3 8 9 10 15 16 17

A) 18 B) 19 C) 20 D) 21 E) 22

4. 40 39 38 36 35 34 32 31 ?

A) 30 B) 29 C) 33 D) 28 E) 27

5. 12 4 18 4 24 4 30 4 ?

A) 4 B) 36 C) 37 D) 38 E) 39

6. 5 14 6 15 7 16 8 17 ?

A) 18 B) 10 C) 19 D) 9 E) 20

7. **1.1** **2.1** **3.1** **4.1** **5.1** **6.1** **7.1** **?**

(A) 7.5   (B) 8.0   (C) 8.1   (D) -45   (E) 9.5

8. **20** **22** **29** **31** **38** **40** **47** **49** **?**

(A) 56   (B) 58   (C) 59   (D) 60   (E) 57

9. **15** **17** **23** **25** **31** **33** **39** **41** **?**

(A) 50   (B) 49   (C) 52   (D) 47   (E) 54

10. **90** **82** **75** **69** **64** **60** **57** **55** **?**

(A) 54   (B) 53   (C) 52   (D) 51   (E) 50

11. **10** **3** **11** **4** **12** **5** **13** **6** **14** ?

(A) 16   (B) 8   (C) 15   (D) 9   (E) 7

12. **80** **79** **78** **76** **75** **74** **72** **71** **?**

(A) 70   (B) 69   (C) 73   (D) 68   (E) 67

13   50   -49   48   -47   46   -45   44   ?

A -42   B -43   C -44   D -44   E -46

14   10   21   15   26   20   31   25   36   ?

A 47   B 37   C 42   D 43   E 30

15   20   0   10   20   0   10   20   ?

A 40   B 30   C 10   D 20   E 0

16   22   21   20   19   18   17   16   ?

A 15   B 14   C 13   D 12   E 11

17   15   3   20   3   25   3   30   3   ?

A 32   B 33   C 34   D 35   E 36

NUMBER ANALOGIES

Directions: The first set and second set of numbers go together in some way. Both of these sets must go together in the <u>same</u> way. Look at the third set where there is a question mark. What number should go here so that all three sets of numbers go together in the same way?

1

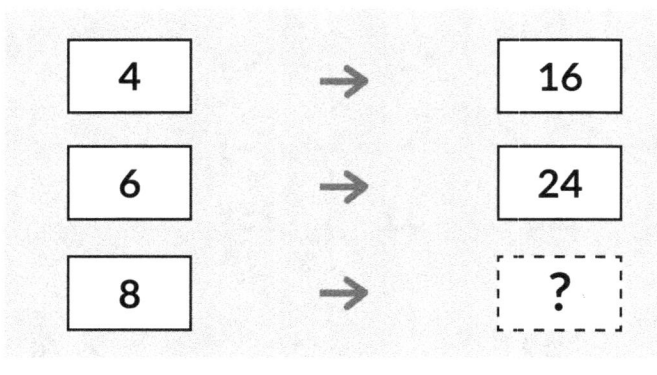

   (A) 20   (B) 32   (C) 34   (D) 4   (E) 12

2

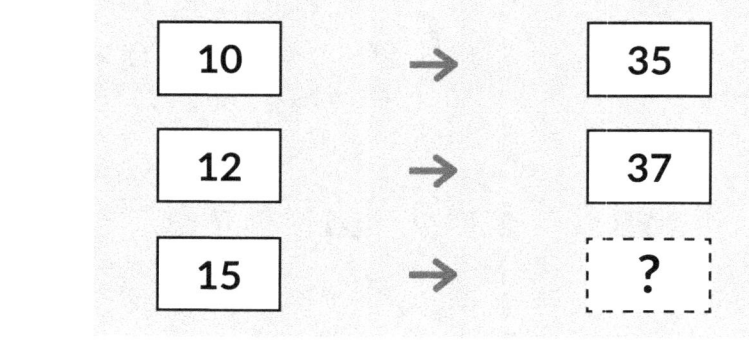

   (A) 40   (B) 42   (C) 43   (D) 44   (E) 25

3

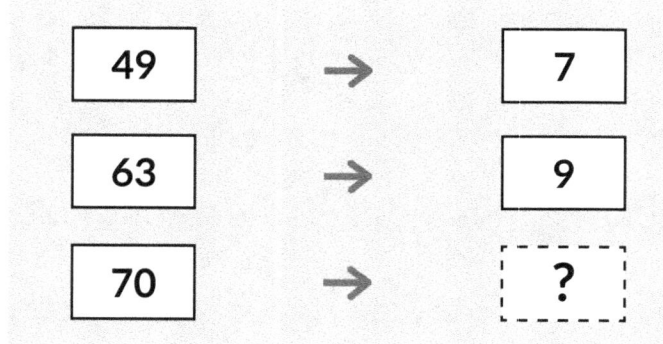

   (A) 7   (B) 28   (C) 10   (D) 11   (E) 63

4

5	→	10
8	→	13
10	→	?

A 20   B 30   C 16   D 17   E 15

5

3	→	15
4	→	20
5	→	?

A 22   B 5   C 10   D 25   E 17

6

19	→	10
17	→	8
16	→	?

A 7   B 8   C 9   D 10   E 11

7   [20 → 40]   [30 → 60]   [25 → ?]

   A) 30   B) 45   C) 55   D) 65   E) 50

8   [9 → 29]   [11 → 31]   [14 → ?]

   A) 24   B) 20   C) 42   D) 34   E) 44

9   [10 → 90]   [5 → 45]   [2 → ?]

   A) 9   B) 29   C) 82   D) 18   E) 20

10   [64 → 8]   [56 → 7]   [72 → ?]

   A) 6   B) 8   C) 9   D) 10   E) 11

11   [81 → 9]   [72 → 8]   [63 → ?]

   A) 6   B) 7   C) 8   D) 9   E) 10

12   [30 → 17]   [24 → 11]   [20 → ?]

   A) 33   B) 13   C) 8   D) 9   E) 7

13   [11 → 31]   [15 → 35]   [0 → ?]

A 25   B 10   C 20   D 55   E 56

14   [5 → 45]   [7 → 63]   [9 → ?]

A 72   B 75   C 81   D 83   E 90

15   [12 → 96]   [10 → 80]   [9 → ?]

A 93   B 81   C 98   D 75   E 72

16   [32 → 4]   [72 → 9]   [56 → ?]

A 6   B 7   C 8   D 28   E 10

17   [26 → 13]   [42 → 21]   [22 → ?]

A 9   B 10   C 11   D 12   E 20

18   [70 → 57]   [43 → 30]   [28 → ?]

A 10   B 13   C 15   D 16   E 20

- End of Practice Test 2 -
- The Answer Key begins on the next page. -

ANSWER KEY FOR PRACTICE TEST 1 (WORKBOOK FORMAT)

Verbal Analogies, Practice Test 1

1. D. The eye is used to see. The ear is used to hear.
2. A. A tiger is a mammal. An ostrich is a bird.
3. B. A disk is shaped like a circle. A die (dice) is shaped like a cube.
4. C. Corn grows on a stalk. Grapes grow on a vine.
5. E. Distance is measured in meters. Weight is measured in grams.
6. B. A carpenter works with wood. A gardener works with plants.
7. B. Skin covers a human. Bark covers a tree.
8. B. Africa has the Nile River. South America has the Amazon River.
9. A. The base of a building has a basement. The base of a volcano has a crater.
10. D. A sparrow is a small bird; an eagle is a larger bird. A salmon is a small fish; a shark is a larger fish.
11. C. Victory is the opposite of defeat. The truth is the opposite of a lie.
12. D. A carrot and broccoli are both vegetables. A peach and an apple are both fruits.
13. A. A snake is a reptile. A toad is an amphibian.
14. A. A biplane and a jet both travel in air, but a jet holds more people. A canoe and a cruise ship both travel on water, but a cruise ship holds more people.
15. C. A saw is used to cut a tree. A knife is used to cut bread.
16. A. Cotton is used to make a shirt. Rubber is used to make a tire.
17. D. Single means one. Quadruple means four.
18. B. A house has an attic at the top. A mountain has a summit at the top.
19. D. Identical is an antonym of opposite. Frigid is an antonym of tropical.
20. E. A novel is written by an author. A sculpture is made by a sculptor.

———————————————————

Verbal Classification, Practice Test 1

1. C. types of birds
2. E. string instruments
3. D. types of nonfiction writing
4. E. cooking methods
5. B. things you write/draw on
6. A. warm weather clothing
7. B. hand tools
8. C. extreme weather events
9. E. things that are white

Verbal Classification, Practice Test 1, continued

10. A. days of the week
11. D. bodies of water (that are not man-made)
12. E. non-primary colors
13. B. units of length
14. A. words that have to do with beginning
15. E. 3-D geometric shapes
16. E. performances
17. C. having to do with 3
18. D. musicians who play instruments
19. C. circular motions
20. B. types of roads
21. A. countries

Sentence Completion, Practice Test 1

1. B. The kitten is stuck up in the tree. So, the dad had to climb up to get to it.

2. D. A thunderstorm would make it unsafe to go to an outdoor amusement park. "Canceled" means the trip was called off and did not happen.

3. E. The sentence is about the slowest horse, so it makes sense that it would not win. The correct answer is "lose" because a slow horse is unlikely to win a contest.

4. C. A mural is something you create with paint or other similar material.

5. A. The kitten fell asleep, so it was tired/sleepy.

6. D. Old photos help us picture the past. "Imagine" means to picture in your mind.

7. C. Someone who refuses new foods is picky. "Picky" means very selective, often refusing things.

8. E. The lifeguard used the whistle to tell the swimmers they needed to get out. "Warning" means telling someone to be careful or to stop because something is about to happen.

9. D. The bird was injured, so they wanted to take care of it. Using a blanket helps keep the bird warm, which is important when it's hurt and waiting for help. The other choices don't match the idea of keeping it safe and warm.

10. A. In spelling bees, contestants repeat words before spelling them. "Repeat" means to say again. The contestants would not have done any of the other choices during a spelling bee.

11. B. James was tired, but he still finished his project. That means he managed to do it, even though it was hard. "Managed" means you were able to do something difficult. The clue is the phrase "even though he was tired," which shows it wasn't easy.

12. C. A path is a narrow way. Hikers would not walk through the forest using any of the other choices.

Sentence Completion, Practice Test 1, continued

13. E. Acorns are produced by oak trees. Acorns grow on oak trees. (Acorns are not flowers, so they do not bloom.)

14. C. A magician wants people to have fun and enjoy the show. That's why the right answer is "entertain." To entertain means to make people smile, laugh, or stay interested in what you're doing.

15. A. "Destroy" means to ruin something completely. They were afraid a strong wave would wash away/destroy the sandcastle. The castle would be gone and could not be fixed.

16. D. The teacher tried to help the student feel better. "Comfort" means to soothe or calm.

17. E. Cold air coming in from outside would make the inside of the house colder. "Lower" means to make something go down, like the temperature.

18. C. Cleaning an attic takes a lot of effort. "Difficult" means hard to do. Cleaning an attic is not something that would be joyful, creative, secret, or lucky.

19. B. A pilot has to pay close attention. "Alert" means watching carefully and ready to act.

20. D. She had less time, so she needed to make her song shorter. "Shorten" means to make something shorter in length or time.

Figure Analogies, Practice Test 1

1. D. The top and middle shapes switch position.

2. E. The colors, black and gray, switch.

3. A. The shape rotates 90 degrees clockwise.

4. E. The color/designs of the large and 2 smaller shapes switch. Also, the 2 smaller shapes align horizontally.

5. B. The last shape becomes the first shape.

6. A. The last shape becomes the first shape.

7. D. On top, a gray diamond changes to a white heart & a white heart changes to a gray diamond. On bottom, the shape switches color (white becomes gray and gray becomes white).

8. E. A smaller version of the outer shape is added to the middle.

9. C. The middle shape rotates 180 degrees. The colors of the 2 shapes switch.

10. D. The shapes align vertically. Inside the 2 shapes that are the same, white changes to dots & dots change to white. The gray arrow rotates 180 degrees to point left.

11. B. The larger outer shape becomes the smallest inner shape. The smallest inner shape becomes the larger outer shape.

12. E. A shape with 1 more side appears. (3 sides become 4 sides on top; 5 sides become 6 sides on the bottom.)

13. A. The number of arrow points is the same number of sides that the shape has, 4 on top and 5 on the bottom.

14. D. The small shapes move inside the gray square as close to their previous positions.

15. B. The top left and bottom right shape switch positions.

16. C. The figures rotate 90 degrees clockwise, and 1 more line group is added.

17. C. The figure rotates 180 degrees.

18. C. The 4-sided shape changes from dark gray to light gray on top & light gray to dark gray on bottom. The small star on the lower left moves to the upper right and becomes a circle. This shape also changes color from light gray to dark gray on top & from dark gray to light gray on bottom.

19. E. The smaller shape moves from the left corner of the larger shape to the right corner. The diagonal lines inside the smaller shape change direction.

Figure Classification, Practice Test 1

1. A. The shapes have vertical lines inside.

2. D. The shapes are round.

3. D. The shapes have diagonal lines going from upper left to lower right.

4. C. One-fourth of the shape is gray.

5. E. In 2 of the 4 sections of the circle, there's 1 star and 1 heart. These 2 shapes are across from each other, but not next to each other.

6. D. The bottom shape is the same as the top shape, but it has been rotated 90 degrees counter-clockwise.

7. D. In the group of 3 shapes, the 2 shapes that are the same are next to each other.

8. B. There's 1 black shape and 2 white shapes.

9. B. There are 3 shapes in the group.

10. E. There are 3 gray rectangles and 2 white rectangles.

11. A. In the middle of the shape group is a heart.

12. D. The black line is on the same point of the triangle.

13. A. The circles have 2 black bars and 1 gray bar.

14. E. The shape group has 1 large shape in the middle surrounded by 2 smaller versions of the same shape.

15. C. The half circles alternate colors, white and gray.

16. B. Each shape group has 1 heart, 1 hexagon, and 1 rectangle. Also, 1 shape is gray, 1 shape is white, and 1 is filled with diagonal lines.

17. A. In each divided square section is a small gray shape. There are two sets of the same shape opposite each other.

18. B. In the group of 3 shapes, there is 1 gray heart and 2 white shapes.

19. A. In the group of 2 shapes, the inner shape has 1 more side than the outer shape.

Paper Folding, Practice Test 1

1. B.	2. D.	3. A.	4. E.	5. C.	6. B.	7. E.
8. D.	9. A.	10. B.	11. E.	12. A.	13. C.	14. D.
15. E.						

Number Puzzles, Practice Test 1

1. C.
2. D.
3. A.
4. B.
5. E.
6. A.
7. C.
8. D.
9. C.
10. C.
11. B.
12. E.
13. A.
14. B.
15. B.
16. C.
17. D.

Number Series, Practice Test 1

1. C.
2. C. The pattern repeats: 3 - 4 -5 - 6.
3. D. Every other rod increases by one: 1 - 2 - 3 - 4. Also, every other alternate rod equals 6.
4. B. Every other rod increases by one: 0 - 1 - 2 - 3. Also, every other alternate rod increases by 1: 4 - 5 - 6.
5. A. The pattern repeats: 6 - 3 - 1 - 2.
6. B. Every other rod decreases by one: 7 - 6 - 5 - 4. Also, every other alternate rod decreases by 1: 4 - 3 - 2.
7. D. The pattern repeats: 2 - 0 - 0.
8. C. +4 -OR- with every other number, 8 is added
9. C. +1, +2 -OR- with every other number, 3 is added

10. A. -1, -2 -OR- with every other number, 3 is subtracted
11. B. +2, +3 -OR- with every other number, 5 is added
12. E. +2, then that same number repeats
13. A. -1, -1, -2
14. C. Add 2 -OR- with every other number, 4 is added
15. D. Add 7 -OR- with every other number, 14 is added
16. E. Alternating +5, +10 -OR- with every other number, 15 is added
17. A. +11, -6 -OR- with every other number, 5 is added
18. E. +1, +1, +2
19. D. -2, +1 -OR- with every other number, 1 is subtracted

Number Analogies, Practice Test 1

1. D. Subtract 1
2. A. Multiply by 2
3. C. Add 3
4. B. Multiply by 4
5. A. Subtract 5
6. E. Divide by 3
7. C. Divide by 10
8. D. Add 7
9. C. Divide by 2
10. A. Subtract 10
11. B. Multiply by 3
12. B. Subtract 12
13. E. Square the number (multiply the number by itself)
14. D. Multiply by 2
15. B. Divide by 5
16. C. Add 6
17. A. Subtract 5
18. E. Multiply by 6

ANSWER KEY FOR PRACTICE TEST 2

Verbal Analogies, Practice Test 2

1. B. You write on paper. You paint on canvas.
2. E. You use an umbrella in the rain. You wear a hat in the sun.
3. C. Morning is to evening as spring is to summer—both are transitions in time/seasons. Evening comes after morning. Summer comes after spring.
4. E. The tool you use to paint is a brush. The tool you use to sew is a needle.
5. C. A captain steers a ship. A pilot flies a jet.
6. A. A dolphin and whale are both large mammals that live in the ocean. A cheetah and lion are both large mammals (and cats) that live mainly in Africa.
7. C. A ruby is a type of gem. Gold is a type metal.
8. A. A horse moves by galloping. A snake moves by slithering.
9. B. A harp is a musical instrument. An oak is a type of tree.
10. C. A year is made up of months. An hour is made up of minutes.
11. B. A glove goes on a hand. A sock goes on a foot.
12. D. The sound an owl makes is a hoot. The sound a lion makes is a roar.
13. E. A teacher is in charge of a classroom. A chef is in charge of a kitchen.
14. A. A coach leads a team. A principal leads a school.
15. D. Narrow is the opposite of wide. Shallow is the opposite of deep.
16. E. A painter creates a painting. A poet creates a poem.
17. C. The Arctic is home to a polar bear. The desert is home to a camel.
18. E. Mouse becomes mice in its plural form. Person becomes people in its plural form.
19. C. An inventor creates an invention. An author creates a book.
20. B. Furious is a stronger form of angry. Exhausted is a stronger form of tired.
21. C. The sole is the bottom of a shoe. The trunk is the bottom of a tree.

Verbal Classification, Practice Test 2

1. E. parts of legs
2. D. types of quadrilaterals (4-sided shapes)
3. D. types of trees
4. A. types of organs
5. A. types of forward movements
6. B. foods that grow underground

Verbal Classification, Practice Test 2, continued

7. C. types of materials/fabrics

8. C. planets

9. E. healthcare professions

10. B. types of vocal expressions/talking

11. B. types of buildings (not parts of buildings)

12. A. types of body coverings that animals have

13. D. fruit that grows on trees

14. C. birds of prey

15. D. hot foods usually eaten with a spoon

16. E. parts of a car necessary for it to function (a radio is not necessary)

17. B. plants

18. B. circular shapes

19. C. body joints

20. E. quiet sounds

Sentence Completion, Practice Test 2

1. C. You mix ingredients together in a bowl. "Blend" means to mix things into one.

2. E. A championship is between people/groups trying to win. "Opponents" are people or teams playing against each other.

3. A. The farther into the forest, the less sunlight because the trees blocked the sunlight. "Disappear" means to go away so you can't see it anymore.

4. B. Cream is something you put on a cut. "Apply" means to put something on a surface. A nurse would not measure, discover, or invent a cream. They may discard (throw out) a cream, but that would not help a cut heal faster.

5. D. A lid keeps steam inside. "Trap" means to keep something from escaping.

6. B. Ice appears when it's freezing. "Form" means to take shape or come together.

7. C. When balloons are inflated (blown up), they need to be tied or they'll float away.

8. D. "Method" means a way of doing something.

9. A. If there are more kids in the art club, then you need to bring more paint brushes because more kids will need a brush.

10. E. The sentence says the players speak other languages, so the rules need to be changed into a language they can understand. "Translate" means to change words from one language into another.

11. C. A thunderstorm can change things fast. "Sudden" means happening quickly.

12. D. Lungs and heart are needed to live. "Necessary" means something you must have.

Sentence Completion, Practice Test 2

13. C. You need water on hot days. "Essential" means very important or needed. If you are hiking outside on a hot day, you must have water because your body needs it to stay cool, have fluids, and not get overheated.

14. A. Judges watch the skaters and decide how well they did. "Assess" means to look at something carefully and say how good or bad it is.

15. E. The sentence says the person wasn't playing, so they were just watching. "Spectator" means someone who watches an event but doesn't take part in it.

16. C. The sentence told us that the books were very popular, so when new ones came in, people quickly bought them. "Arrived" means they got there, and "purchased" means bought.

17. D. They thought traffic would be a problem. "Expected" means thought something would happen.

18. D. The overview is short. "Brief" means not long.

19. A. If something irritates your eyes, that means it bothers or hurts it. So if the drops cause a problem, you shouldn't use them again. "Irritate" means to make something itchy, sore, or uncomfortable.

20. E. The sentence shows that the weather can change, so you need to be ready for hot or cold. "Unpredictable" means you don't know what will happen next.

Figure Analogies, Practice Test 2

1. A. The figure "flips" to become a mirror image of the original version.

2. E. The colors switch.

3. C. The larger shape remains and has the color of the smaller shape.

4. D. The figure "flips" to become a mirror image of the original version.

5. D. One more smaller shape is added.

6. B. The shape group rotates 180 degrees and the designs inside (gray or dotted) switch.

7. E. The circles change like this: circles with lines become light gray circles, gray circles become circles filled with lines, dark gray circles become circles filled with wavy lines, and circles with wavy lines become dark gray.

8. C. The first shape (a triangle/a trapezoid) rotates 90 degrees clockwise and appears inside a parallelogram.

9. D. All shapes switch color from gray to black/black to gray. The smallest center shape & large outer shape switch positions. Also, the middle shape becomes slightly smaller.

10. A. The shape group rotates 180 degrees & switches color (gray and white). On top, the octagon rotates 180 degrees, but because of the octagon's dimensions, the rotated octagon looks exactly the same as the original. When the triangle rotates 180 degrees, you can see that it changes from pointing up to pointing down.

11. E. The inside shape changes to a shape that has one more side. The outside shape changes to a shape with one more side. The shapes switch colors (dark gray and light gray).

12. B. The top shape becomes larger. There are 2 of the same bottom shapes inside this larger shape. They are next to each other and face opposite directions.

13. E. The white arrow shape rotates 180 degrees. The colors inside the 3 circles switch (dark gray and light gray).

14. D. The bottom shape rotates 180 degrees. The top and bottom shape switch colors. Also, the top and bottom shape move next to each other.

15. C. The figure "flips" and becomes a mirror image of the original version.

16. B. The middle shape becomes the largest, outer shape. Then, the top shape becomes larger and moves inside the outer shape. Then, the bottom shape moves inside both of these shapes. It also rotates 180 degrees & turns gray.

17. E. The shapes change like this: the arrows pointing right become light gray squares, the arrows pointing down become dark gray triangles, and the arrows pointing up become dark gray ovals.

18. B. Notice the black sections of the "X" and the "O." They change like this: X with upper left shaded = O with upper right shaded; X with upper right shaded = O with upper left shaded; X with lower left shaded = O with lower right shaded; X with lower right shaded = O with lower left shaded.

Figure Classification, Practice Test 2

1. E. The shapes have 8 sides.

2. B. Half of the shape is black. Half of the shape is white.

3. A. The 3 circles form 3-in-a-row (tic-tac-toe), plus 1 half-circle that is not directly next to any of the circles.

4. C. There is a shape in the upper left corner of the hexagon. This shape is a different color from the hexagon.

5. D. Inside 2 of the circles is a heart and a star. These 2 shapes are next to each other (not across).

6. C. The middle shape has horizontal lines inside it.

7. E. As the shape group rotates, the circle remains at the same position on the white "L". The shape group rotates 90 degrees counter-clockwise each time.

8. B. Inside the divided larger shape is: 1 heart, 1 star, and 1 half-circle.

9. B. There are 3 small circles: 1 is black, 1 is white, and 1 is gray.

10. D. In the group of 3 shapes, 1 has dots, 1 is gray, and 1 is white. Also, 1 shape is a hexagon, 1 is a pentagon, and 1 is a cube.

11. E. One section of the divided shape has 1 white shape that's a smaller version of the larger shape.

12. A. The large triangle has horizontal lines inside. The black and small white shapes are not the same kind of shape. (Choice C is not the correct answer because inside, the 2 shapes are the same.)

Figure Classification, Practice Test 2, continued

13. E. In each shape group there is: 1 gray shape, 1 white shape, 1 black shape. The shapes must align diagonally (not vertically or horizontally).

14. C. The largest shape and smallest shape have the same design or color. The 3 shapes must be different shapes.

15. A. The shape group rotates 90 degrees clockwise each time.

16. D. The shapes have a diagonal line going from upper left to lower right.

17. B. The shapes have 5 sides.

18. E. The shapes have 2 dividing lines. One line is perfectly vertical. One line is perfectly horizontal.

Paper Folding, Practice Test 2

1. A.	2. B.	3. E.	4. D.	5. E.	6. C.	7. D.
8. A.	9. B.	10. E.	11. C.	12. C.	13. A.	14. B.

Number Puzzles, Practice Test 2

1. B.	2. E.	3. C.	4. B.	5. D.	6. A.	7. D.
8. B.	9. C.	10. C.	11. A.	12. E.	13. E.	14. B.
15. D.	16. C.	17. B.	18. A.			

Number Patterns, Practice Test 2

1. E. subtracting by increasing digits: −1, −2, −3, etc.

2. C. repeat: 5, 10, 20

3. E. +1, +1, +5; +1, +1, +5, repeats

4. A. -1, -1, -2; -1, -1, -2, repeats

5. B. every other number increases by 6; every alternate number is 4

6. D. every other number increases by 1: 5, 6, 7, 8; every alternate number increases by 1: 14, 15, 16, 17

7. C. +1.0

8. A. +2, then +7 -OR- every other number increases by 9

9. D. +2, then +6 -OR- every other number increases by 8

10. A. subtract by decreasing digits: -8, -7, -6, -5, etc.

11. E. every other number increases by 1 (10, 11, 12, 13, 14) & every alternate number increases by 1 (3, 4, 5, 6, 7) -OR- there's a difference of 7 between every set of numbers (10, 3) and (11, 4)

Number Patterns, Practice Test 2, continued

12. A. -1, -1, -2; -1, -1, -2, repeats

13. B. the signs alternate positive and negative -and- the digits decrease by 1

14. E. +11, -6, +11, -6

15. E. 20, 0, 10, repeats

16. A. every other number (22, 20, 18, 16) decreases by 2 -and- every other number (21, 19, 17, and 15) decreases by 2 -OR- there's a difference of 1 between every set of numbers (22 and 21), (20 and 19)

17. D. every other number increases by 5 -and- every other number is a 3

Number Analogies, Practice Test 2

1. B. x4   2. A. +25   3. C. ÷7   4. E. +5
5. D. ×5   6. A. −9   7. E. ×2   8. D. +20
9. D. ×9   10. C. ÷8   11. B. ÷9   12. E. −13
13. C. +20   14. C. ×9   15. E. ×8   16. B. ÷8
17. C. ÷2   18. C. −13

Need more practice?

• Get **300+ <u>new</u> questions** per book!

• Check out more **Savant Test Prep**™ books on Amazon®.